ENCOUNTER
WITH
GOD
IN
JOB

ENCOUNTER
WITH
GOD
IN
JOB

DENNIS LENNON

SERIES EDITORS
ALISON BARR, JOSEPHINE CAMPBELL, TONY HOBBS

SCRIPTURE UNION
130 CITY ROAD LONDON EC1V 2NJ

First published 1995

ISBN 0 86201 946 X

British Library Cataloguing-in-Publication Data
A catalogue record for this book is available from the British Library.

Cover design by Grax Design Consultants.

Phototypeset by Intype, London.
Printed and bound in Great Britain by Cox & Wyman Ltd, Reading, Berkshire.

CONTENTS

FOREWORD

Throughout its long history, promoting systematic, daily Bible reading has always been central to Scripture Union's world-wide ministry. At first there were Bible-reading cards that detailed a series of daily readings throughout the year. But before too long comments were published to accompany the notes and, in the early 1920s, a quarterly booklet was produced. It was called *The Scripture Union* with the sub-title 'Daily Notes', the name by which the booklet was to become known

By the 1990s Scripture Union's promotion of systematic daily Bible reading relied on three separate Bible-reading notes for the English-speaking world. Like *Daily Notes, Daily Bread* was widely used over several decades and these two were joined more recently by *Alive to God* which was launched to offer a complementary approach to Bible reading. All three publications have always had the following in common:

A commitment to the authority and inspiration of
biblical text;
A conviction that reading the Bible should not
merely be a cerebral process; the reader should
also be encouraged to respond to what they
have read.

Bible-reading notes inevitably reflect the culture and concerns of their time. So, for example, some of the early notes made frequent attempts to summarise biblical passages using three points. Although this was a useful *aide-mémoire*, it did tend to be somewhat forced at times! More interestingly, the notes of the '30s, '40s and '50s – when the evangelical world was struggling with the impact of the implications of liberal scholarship – concentrated on re-stating the basic doctrinal truths. Today the notes reflect a strong emphasis on the importance of applying biblical principles, and the growing interest throughout the Christian world on what can be described as 'spirituality'. This is seen in the increasingly varied forms of worship, the rediscovery of ancient Christian writing and music, and an awareness that responding to God can involve feelings and emotions as well as the mind.

There is much in Christian culture that is exciting and refreshing, but it is taking place against a background of a widespread decrease in Bible reading. It seems that the emphasis on Christian experience – important as that is – is blinding many people to the other side of the Christian life: duty and discipline. Twenty years ago most members of evangelical churches were committed to the importance of personal Bible reading on a regular basis. Nowadays, although many churches would claim to be Bible based, individual members have all too often given up regular personal Bible reading. Bible-reading aids cannot in themselves change this trend. What we must continue to pray for is God's Holy Spirit to provoke whole Christian communities to rediscover the importance and excitement of regular Bible reading – without losing the joy of the variety and depth of Christian experience.

Marrying regular Bible reading with dynamic Christian experience is the aim of Scripture Union Bible-reading notes. Partly to reflect that principle, it was recently decided to change the title of *Daily Notes* to *Encounter With God*. The former described the process but the latter describes the purpose.

Over the years readers have often encouraged us to reprint popular series of the notes. However, we have always been reluctant to do so, partly because writers prepare notes prayerfully and under the guidance of the Holy Spirit for use at a particular time and in a particular way. Numerous stories from readers testify to how a particular note on a particular day met a specific need, and are witnesses to the Holy Spirit's role in the process. Nevertheless, when in the early 1990s we began to deal with entire biblical books in a single series, a formula began to suggest itself: not a reprinting of the series as such, but the series re-worked and expanded by the writer; still using the distinctive *Encounter With God* approach, but with the space to develop and explore some of the issues which could not be covered in a 300–word note.

There are a number of things that make Scripture Union Bible-reading notes distinctive, but one element perhaps stands out above all others: beginning and ending with scripture. Starting with the Bible passage, the writer offers thought-provoking comments to encourage the reader to go back to the passage with fresh enthusiasm and new insights, eager to respond with new commitment to what God is saying through scripture: in other words, *to encounter God*. It is the prayer of all who have worked on this series that such will be your experience as you read this book.

Tony Hobbs
Commissioning Editor
Adult Bible Reading Publications

INTRODUCTION

The book of *Job* is not for the squeamish. It is a storming, laughing, raging, mocking, sarcastic, weeping, praying, near-blasphemous, worshipping book. The language is beautiful and violent, haunting and a slap in the face, ecstatic and deranged. Above all, it is mostly poetry, pouring out of the author's innermost being, full of stunning images and metaphors and parables. Its pace, voltage and energy matches its subject: a godly man struggling with the spiritual despair of cruel, undeserved suffering. Job is, in that sense, Everyman in that suffering is our fundamental human condition.

In terms of ideas, *Job* belongs to that period in the Old Testament when God's people were compelled by the bitter experiences of defeat and captivity in Babylon to seek radically new interpretations of their relationship with God and his world. What Isaiah does for Israel Job does for the individual. He is a product of the 'wisdom' school, whose philosophers gave us *Proverbs* and *Ecclesiastes* – writings which have remarkably little to say about the problems of innocent suffering and the mystery of God's providence.

Job is a man who finds that the teachings of the wisdom tradition do not cover the facts of his new, terrible experiences. His friends are committed to the old understanding of the tight, unbreakable connection between sin and suffering, or good works and prosperity. Their conclusion is that Job is suffering because sin is present somewhere in his life or in the life of his family. Job fights his way out of that system of thought to seek a radically different explanation, one that matches reality. And all the time God remains silent: Job is allowed to slog through the marshlands of his loneliness, illness and anger against the God who, for some unknown reason, has turned against him. The answer Job arrives at by the end of his journey will involve us in a thrilling vision of the world and invite us into an astonishing spiritual experience.

This book will, I hope, draw the shortest and straightest possible line between Job and our own present situation. It is not a commentary but an aid to thought, meditation, prayer and decision. We will work through *Job* section by section, looking to find the heart and centre of gravity of each. There is tremendous value in reading through the book in that way rather than by, for example, selecting themes. *Job* offers startling insights – often unusual insights for readers who are more at home in the New Testament – which come spinning out in all directions. These may have the effect of forcing open our vision and wonderfully enlarging and enriching our spiritual awareness. We must give them their full value, however awkwardly they sit in relation to our doctrinal ideas and however uncomfortable they make us feel. Refuse the temptation to tone them down, smooth their edges, render them more tame and manageable. On the contrary, be open to the possibility of becoming more 'semitic', imaginative, creative in your thought-world and in your prayer vocabulary.

THE WAGER

Job 1 – 2:10

Imagine an argument in heaven. Satan is there in his role as chief global snooper (Job 1:6,7). His report this time is an absolute bombshell. If what he says is true then the Creator's purpose in creating has run into serious trouble. Satan produces his evidence. War? Famine? Aids? No, but a condition endemic in the human race which, he claims, discredits God as the wise Creator: *there is no sincere love for God on the earth*. The angels look on anxiously.

'Wrong,' God answers, 'and here is someone to prove you wrong: Job, a man of complete integrity, who is sincerely committed to me' (v8).

Satan will have none of it. 'Does Job fear God for nothing?' he sneers (v9). Any creature will lick the hand that feeds it. It is merely 'cupboard love'. Job's famous piety is a barter-religion. God has his vote because God is so generous to him. Job does not want God, but only his goods.

Satan has the same sour opinion of us, but then that is his nature.

> I met the Devil too
> And the adjectives by which I would describe him
>   are these:
> Solemn
> Boring
> Conservative . . .

Got into a rage when someone laughed;
He was serious about unserious things;
You had to be careful about his inferiority complex
For he was conscious of being uncreative.
                                        Patrick Kavanagh[1]

Satan is an astute theologian, whatever else he may be.
He knows full well what would pull the linchpin out of
the created order. God is love and everywhere his works
express his nature. He desires to bring into being sons and
daughters in his own image who are free to know and love
him. Marvellous creatures, these human beings, unique in
their spiritual-bodily nature. They stand half-way between
heaven and earth, at one with the physical world, yet all
the time heading for eternity where they will see the face
of God. They mediate between the Creator and his work.
Alone of all creatures on the earth they have the mysterious
gift of speech by which to release inarticulate nature to
join in the cosmic celebration of God. Adam named each
thing, thus freeing it from suffocating confusion to take
its rightful place in the great scheme of things (Genesis
2:19,20; Hebrews 2:5–8).

Onely to Man thou hast made known thy wayes,
And put the penne alone into his hand,
And made him Secretarie of thy praise.
                                        George Herbert[2]

Love flowing freely and delightfully between God and his
children is at the heart of the mystery of God's relationship
with the world. 'His plans for us are what perfect wisdom
suggests to infinite love,' wrote Austin Farrer.[3] Our love,
praise and awe vindicate the wisdom of the Creator. And
in choosing God we are most true to our own nature,
never more free to be ourselves than when dedicated to
our Father's good pleasure.

Satan's claim is that he has looked closely but cannot
find such God-adoring human beings. If the measure of a

good world is true devotion and sincere love for God, then creation must be reckoned a flop. He could quote scripture (future scripture!) to support his argument: 'If I ... have not love, I am nothing ... Love never fails ... And now these three remain: faith, hope and love. But the greatest of these is love' (1 Corinthians 13). Without love nothing stands, the reason for our existence is ripped out. Or, to reverse that nightmare scenario, God the Holy Trinity will live with the person who loves (John 14:23)

Our beautiful liturgies and exuberant praise gatherings, even our sacrificial service, leave the cynical principalities and powers unimpressed: 'Do they worship God for nothing?' Just give that congregation, or this Christian, a poke with a sharp stick and you will see their devotion evaporating in confusion and despair. Before long you will hear them whinge and mutter as they pack their bags and go off in search of a more reasonable God. '*Love is not love which alters when it alteration finds ...* '[4] There is enough in Satan's accusation to disturb any believer. We can say several things ...

The love

We can admit that Satan is basically correct in his analysis of our defective love for the Lord. Admit it, and repent of it. Which of us could deny our drift into hypocrisy, the double-mindedness that is play-acting? We use and exploit God's love. At heart we want a 'heavenly butler' of the Jeeves school, who glides in with a whisky and soda just when we need it and silently slips out again until the next crisis. In his lovely poem, 'Unkindnesse', George Herbert admits to a callous indifference to God's love, ending with the comment:

> My God upon a tree
> His bloud did spill
> Onely to purchase my good-will:
> Yet use I not my foes, as I use thee.

Can we get to the truth about ourselves given that we are, for the most part, so adept at self-deception? Endless introspection, everlastingly peeling the psychological onion of motives, is a futile and depressing exercise. Better to keep it short and sharp, simple and straight, taking the will of God into account and letting the Holy Spirit orchestrate your desires and actions *now.* Is he telling you to do something, or to cease from doing something, maybe with regard to your money, ambition or marriage? Then prove the sincerity of your love for God by doing it, or not doing it, as he commands. 'If you love me keep my commandments,' Jesus said. Prolonged investigation may be just a smoke screen for procrastination or downright disobedience. The Spirit is at work within you to heal your many-mindedness, to make you one person, organised around the one, burning centre of his love.

Does Satan know anything about sincere love? Why should we credit him with the possibility? The perverted demonic mind cannot imagine a love which is 'for nothing' (v9). He would not recognise the genuine thing if he saw it. In what must be still the most perceptive exposition of satanic attitudes – *The Screwtape Letters* by C S Lewis[5] – Screwtape writes to the apprentice demon, his young nephew Wormwood:

> To us a human is primarily food; our aim is the absorption of its will into ours, the increase of our own area of selfhood at its expense. But the obedience which the Enemy [that is, God] demands of men is quite a different thing. One must face the fact that all the talk about His love for men, and His service being perfect freedom, is not (as one would gladly believe) mere propaganda, but an appalling truth. He really *does* want to fill the universe with a lot of loathsome little replicas of Himself – creatures whose life, on its miniature scale, will be qualitatively like His own, not because He

has absorbed them but because their wills freely
conform to His. We want cattle who can finally
become food; He wants servants who can finally
become sons. We want to suck in, He wants to give
out. We are empty and would be filled; He is full
and flows over. Our war aim is a world in which Our
Father Below has drawn all other beings into himself;
the Enemy wants a world full of beings united to
Him but still distinct.

Although Screwtape rashly concedes the reality of God's
love for his children, on reflection the demonic mind
cannot bring itself to believe it possible. There must be
another explanation:

> The truth is I slipped by mere carelessness into saying
> that the Enemy really loves the humans. That, of
> course, is an impossibility ... All His talk about love
> must be disguise for something else – He must have
> some *real* motive for creating them and taking so
> much trouble about them. The reason one comes
> to talk as if He really had this impossible Love is
> our utter failure to find out that real motive. What
> does He stand to make out of them? That is the
> insoluble question.

Satan questions Job's motives for his devotion to God,
Screwtape questions God's motives for loving Job. Driven
by suspicion and scorn, the enemy hates the overflow of
divine love drenching our hearts – 'I have loved you with
an everlasting love ...' (Jeremiah 31:3) – and our grateful
love reaching out to him in response through Jesus Christ
– 'Though you have not seen him, you love him ... and
are filled with an inexpressible and glorious joy' (1 Peter
1:8).

Of course, true love brings benefits along with it. We feel
the *need* to love. It gives us joy. 'But I do love thee! and

when I love thee not Chaos is come again' was Othello's famous description of the way things are for lovers. But the reverse is not true. If I said I wanted to avoid chaos in my life by deciding to love my wife, I would soon find that the chemistry did not work, that my decision smacked of the ulterior motives of cupboard love.

Are we right to use 'in love'-type language for the believer's relationship with God? Why not? Scripture and Christian tradition are full of it. In *Hosea* the heart-broken God is betrayed repeatedly by his 'flighty wife', Israel. And how else are we to understand Solomon's *Song of Songs*? Surely it is more than just an ancient manual of courtship. 'Do the great lovers of God who turn to the Song of Songs do so merely to use the rhetoric of love? No, they are drawn to it because it is the very source of that rhetoric. Without it they would be mute,' writes Barry Ulanov.[6] It is significant that the final, and therefore the ultimate, picture of God's people in perfect communion with him is as 'a bride beautifully dressed for her husband' (Revelation 21:1,2).

Jewish writings since the biblical period, steeped in the ancient imagery of the love affair between God and Israel, speak extensively in similar metaphors. In the beautiful 'Song at Daybreak'[7] the worshipper starts the day in the presence of God:

> Take care of the soul: she is turquoise, agate, and jasper. Her light is like the light of the sun, like the light of seven mornings at once . . .

> May [God] find her wrapped in prayer-shawl and frontlets, always dressed like a bride, morning after morning.

Language climbs to a higher voltage in Christian devotion, as in John Donne's passionate and daring outburst:[8]

Take me to you, imprison me, for I
Except you enthrall me, never shall be free,
Nor ever chaste, except you ravish me.

An over-intellectualised faith will be embarrassed by out-
pourings of this kind. Yet it is the glory and the beauty of
the One addressed which saves Donne's language from
sliding into a swooning, sentimental, near-eroticism. Christ
is the 'desire of nations'. Evangelists remark that while
people do come to faith through an explanation of the
gospel that satisfies the intellect, many others are simply
drawn to the man Jesus. They respond to him because he
appears to them as utterly desirable and believable. There
may follow a level of whole-hearted commitment to Christ
out of all proportion to the theological understanding of
the new believer. So, yes, for many people the analogy
with falling in love is a fair one. 'The heart has its reasons
of which reason knows nothing' (Pascal).

But what do I love in loving you?
Not physical beauty,
nor transitory charm,
nor the splendour of light
which is so dear to my eyes;
not the sweet melodies of many songs;
nor the perfume of flowers, ointments and spices;
not manna
nor honey;
not the delights of physical embrace.
In loving my God
I do not love such things.
Yet in loving him
I nonetheless love a certain light, a voice, a perfume,
food and an embrace deep within my being:
where my soul is bathed
in a light which no place can contain,
where a voice is heard
that no passage of time

can ever remove,
where a fragrance abounds
that no gust of winds can disperse,
where there is a savour
that no ravenous hunger can diminish,
where there is an embrace
that no fulfilment can bring to an end.
This is what I love
when I love my God.

Augustine[9]

The glory of the New Covenant which Jesus administrates between God and ourselves is that the Holy Spirit implants within us the new heart and new desires which make us want to want God (Hebrews 9:15). To our astonishment we prove the truth of the promise 'Delight yourself in the Lord and he will give you the desires of your heart' (Psalm 37:4). The miracle is that we find ourselves desiring the things that delight the Lord. The Old Covenant never could deliver that marvellous resonance between the heart of God and our hearts. In the New, the Holy Spirit imparts to us the very thing he requires in us. 'I will put my laws in their minds and write them on their hearts. I will be their God and they will be my people' (Hebrews 8:7–13). Penetrating the depths of our psyche, the Spirit pours in the new love of God. The only way to be rid of old sinful loves is by the exorcising power of the new love (Romans 5:5; 8:5,6).

The witness

God has faith in his people. It is a risky position for the Almighty to take, and here he entrusts his reputation to a man: 'Have you considered my servant Job?' (Job 1:8). Throughout scripture the honour and purpose of God ride on one person – Adam, Noah, Abraham, Jesus – or a family, a tribe, a church. They are living, breathing, walking evidence of the divine purpose in the world.

Jesus is called 'the faithful and true witness' (Revelation 3:14) whose character and work testify to the loving wisdom of God: 'Anyone who has seen me has seen the Father' (John 14:9). And we, in our turn, carry his reputation because he claimed that our lives are finally the only apologetic that matters. We are 'salt' and 'light' because we draw from him who is *the* salt and light of the world (Matthew 5:13–16).

'Have you considered my servant...?' Complete the sentence with your own name. As a Christian you carry God's reputation wherever you are. In practice this means that your behaviour should remind people of God as you act in a way characteristic of him. According to second century Diognetus, Christians 'are kept in the world as in a prison-house, and yet they are the ones who hold the world together!' It is clear the Christians of his day carried God's reputation in great style. To be the glue which holds a shattered society together is a profoundly God-like function. These Christians reminded people of God because they did things which were typical of God.

More than anything, this high calling to champion God's reputation in the world bestows immense purpose, value and dignity to our lives whoever we are.

> O let thy sacred will
> All thy delight in me fulfil!
> Let me not think an action mine own way,
> But as thy love shall sway,
> Resigning up the rudder to thy skill.
>
> *George Herbert*[10]

Job, of course, had no idea of the debate going on in heaven. Similarly, for our part we seldom have little more than a glimmer of the spiritual dynamics of the various situations we are in each day. However, what is certain is that we are to witness to the truth of Christ as we receive it. 'You will be my witnesses,' said Jesus (Acts 1:8). 'You are chosen people ... that you may declare the praises of him who called you out of darkness into his wonderful light,' wrote Peter (1 Peter 2:9,10). We are to witness with integrity (Job 2:3). In his advice to Christians who are anxious about witnessing, John White writes:[11]

> To let my light shine demands no more than honesty. It demands honesty before unbelievers. Witnessing is not putting on a Christian front so as to convince prospective customers. Witnessing is being honest, that is being true to what God has made me in my speech and in my day to day behaviour.
>
> ... If we are even partially honest (total honesty is rare and difficult) in a conversation with an unbeliever, we will find it extremely difficult to avoid talking about Christian things. Do you say it is difficult to witness? I maintain that, with a little honesty, it is almost impossible not to witness.

Be honest. God requires no more of us. Be honest to God even in times of suffering. Especially in times of suffering. Satan is sure we will not. 'Does Job fear God for nothing?' Only a searching examination will tell.

The examination

We have come to expect demonic hostility. We understand the reason for it, yet the idea that God steps aside and allows it to happen can be, to say the least, disappointing when we are on the receiving end of satanic attention.

Satan receives God's permission to test Job's sincerity. Scripture is clear: the concept of two competing centres of spiritual power over against each other – light and darkness, good and evil, life and death, God and Satan – is false. No, all things are under God's sway and exist only by his permission, even demonic activity and the dire consequences of human evil. Satan cannot break out and establish a base outside God's sphere of influence. 'I form the light and create darkness, I bring prosperity and create disaster; I, the Lord, do all these things' (Isaiah 45:7).

Although evil has entered the texture of life, God does not therefore undo what he has made, like unpicking the threads of a tapestry. Rather he reveals his sovereignty in compelling evil, and all things in heaven and earth, to serve his redeeming purposes. In Revelation 5:1–9 we read that the book of destiny may be opened only by the one qualified to do so – Christ, the Lamb of God, on the throne. Jesus has authority to hold the principalities and powers on a leash. They too, in being true to their hate-ridden nature, merely manage to serve God's purpose in the end. They are permitted their freedom but within limits (1 Corinthians 10:13; Revelation 12).

> The Christian knows what the world does not know, that it is by the power of God that Satan exists, by his permission that he rebels, and by his will that the kingdom of Messiah subdues him.
>
> *Austin Farrer*[12]

A culture obsessed with 'therapy' like ours in the West cannot cope with talk of this kind. The idea of this life as a place of testing, of soul-making, does not sit easily with a feel-good philosophy of life. But God has far bigger things in mind for us than life perpetually in the Comfort Zone.

Out of a clear blue sky Job's life is laid in ruins by a series of disasters that rob him of his possessions and his children (Job 1:13–19). Will he speak as well of God now as he did in the good days? He responds with a confession of faith – if God gave, then he can also take away (1:21). The accuser's first test fails to break him. However, Satan cynically asserts that Job is an egotist who would, if pushed to the limit, allow others to sacrifice their skin in order to save his own (2:4,5). Attack his health, and his loyalty to God will collapse (2:6–8). Job responds with a second confession: we cannot accept the good from God and refuse the trouble (2:10). Remember, he had no idea that God had already answered on his behalf before all heaven, or that God had placed his own reputation on the line when he backed his man against Satan. Completely in the dark as to the reason for the catastrophe, Job vindicates God's trust by his two confessions. 'He suffers as the glory and pride of God' (Herder). To see a believer steadfast in suffering is impressive, which is not to glorify hardship but simply to state a fact of life. We are, for example, moved and our faith strengthened by the way Russian Christians came through the appalling hardships of the Gulags.

What are the qualities of a person who can carry the 'glory and pride of God' into the darkness of innocent suffering?

Job – the measure of the man

A cluster of words suggest his character (1:1,8; 2:3). The key trait is integrity, from the little Hebrew word *tam* meaning 'whole, sound, complete, unimpaired, healthful'. God chose his man for his personal qualities. Character is rated higher than brain power in the biblical vision of humanity. 'Is she a good person?' is a more biblical question than 'Is she clever?' Character refers to the entire person, whole and unified, organised around one centre. 'The good man brings good things out of the good stored up in him' (Matthew 12:35).

Integrity of character is in itself a witness of God, since God is three persons moving in unity around the common centre of their mutual love. God's true witnesses are people of integrity. They pay for their words with their life-style and, if required, with their lives. They give their word and stand by it. We say, 'She is as good as her word' or, 'We have his word on it'. That is witness-with-integrity: 'doers of the word (of God), not hearers only'.

Our Lord's vivid picture of witness-with-integrity is 'If

anyone would come after me, he must deny himself and take up his cross and follow me' (Mark 8:34). The cross-carrier, in Roman practice, first had to run the gauntlet of the jeering and spiteful crowd. To take up your cross means, therefore, that you will certainly have to go against the crowd and prevailing popular opinions.

At the same time we know from experience the remarkable sense of peace and 'rightness' that is ours when, by the grace of God, we dare to refuse cowardly conformity to popular opinion. Time and again, Jesus appears to his frightened followers with the words 'Peace – be not afraid!' It is a gracious greeting, a blessing, a promise, an invitation, a command even. 'The peace of God' (Philippians 4:3–7) is the source of the power which enables us to go against the flow. Job calls it 'fearing God', an attitude which feeds through into his integrity of faith and life.

Therefore we are *not* talking about natural strength of character or fine intellect, or the beautifully balanced personality some fortunate people are born with. In his second letter Peter urges his readers to seek character from God. People who are by nature timid or indecisive can grow in strength and resolution in Christ. We have received 'everything we need for life and godliness ... Through these he has given us his very great and precious promises, so that through them you may participate in the divine nature ... [making] every effort to add to your faith ...' (2 Peter 1:3–9).

Character becomes godly only through experience. There is no correspondence course available on character building; only life and grace mixed together will do. Under stress we will know if the centre holds, if we will bless God or curse him, if our life has integrity. The New Testament writers positively welcome trials and difficulties, not because they are closet masochists but so that our 'faith – of greater worth than gold, which perishes even though refined by fire – may be proved genuine and may result in praise, glory and honour when Jesus Christ is revealed' (1 Peter 1:7).

The second characteristic of Job is found in the little phrase already mentioned: 'he feared God' (Job 1:1,8,9; 2:3). Fear is one of our fundamental responses to God's demands on us. His transcendent purity and holiness place our sinfulness in perspective. 'Fear and trembling' are entirely appropriate for Christians whose loving heavenly Father is also 'a consuming fire' inspiring 'reverence and awe' (Philippians 2:12; Hebrews 12:28). However, in many societies today materialistic values dominate, and the impact of God, the All Holy One, upon us has been greatly dulled. But Isaiah saw God and was aghast (Isaiah 6). Ezekiel glimpsed his splendour and was 'overwhelmed' for seven days (Ezekiel 3:15). Daniel also was, 'terrified ... exhausted and lay ill ... appalled ... deathly pale ... helpless' (Daniel 8:17,27; 10:8). John saw the glory of the Lord and fainted (Revelation 1:12–17). The fear of God is a fear we cannot live without. It consumes other fears and anxieties, leaving us with this one fear: 'Fear him, ye saints, and you will then have nothing else to fear'. This fear (awe, dread, adoration) puts the whole of life into perspective. It integrates and organises our inner life around reverence for God as the centre of our existence. We can no more snuggle up to *this* God than we could to a nuclear reactor or a starburst.

Frankly, the Hebrew tradition seems to celebrate the awesome transcendent holiness of God more authentically than much of our worship:

> Whoever looks at Him is instantly torn; whoever glimpses His beauty immediately melts away.
> [Lit. 'is emptied out like a ladle'.]

> A quality of holiness, a quality of power, a fearful quality, a dreaded quality, a quality of awe, a quality of shuddering, a quality of dismay, a quality of terror ...[13]

This sounds very much like the experience of Isaiah,

Ezekiel, Daniel and John, and very different from the over-familiar, flip attitudes towards God prevalent today.

Reverence pulls on life like a compass needle swinging around to seek magnetic north each time. Within the mind of a person like Job reverence was a directing power, influencing his imagination and attitudes and giving a distinctive slant to his values, reactions, assessments of life. In Job reverence for God is a habit of mind, as regular as breathing (Job 1:4,5).

A third aspect of Job's character is his wisdom: 'The fear of the Lord – that is wisdom' (28:28). In fact Job was one of the three exemplary wise men of the ancient world (Ezekiel 14:14). Their reverential slant of mind helped them to discern the truth.

Job is wise – his wife is not. She, poor lady, also lost everything when Job's life fell apart. In despair she suggests he terminate the remainder of his existence: 'Curse God and die' (Job 2:9). She talks, says Job, like a 'foolish woman' (v10). This rebuke is a lot heavier than it sounds. 'Foolish' implies a lack of order in a person's innermost being. The 'fool' is basically unsound in his judgement because he does not know what is going on at the centre of events. In fact 'folly' is a form of practical atheism, living life without taking God seriously. The ancients thought the 'fool' unteachable because God was missing from his view of things.

Now we can better appreciate the strong, unyielding simplicity of Job's two confessions (1:21; 2:10). He had taken up a stance about God's goodness and faithfulness which no immediate disaster could shift. Clearly he had made up his mind long since about the way he would speak of God (see Romans 8:31–39). It is a believer's duty to talk with care and reverence about God. Would you habitually speak well of him? Jesus directs your attention to the content, the processes and the interior climate of the heart.

'For out of the overflow of the heart the mouth speaks' (Matthew 12:34).

Job survived his scorching examination. He spoke well of God. His two confessions wiped the sneer off Satan's face. This man *did* fear God 'for nothing' (Job 1:9).

THE FRIENDS

Job 2:11 – 13

Walled in by the strain of prolonged grief and illness, Job needs friends. Real friends are not content to drop a line or fax condolences. They will make every effort to come personally. Job is fortunate in his friends. As we shall see, they often disagree with him, sometimes violently, but they care. They earn the right to talk frankly with him by the sincerity of their friendship.

A repellent sight with his ghastly skin condition, quarantined on his ash-heap, Job needs their company: the sound of their voices, the comfort of their touch. Before words, deeper than words, his friends penetrate his awful isolation with their tears and by tearing their clothes as a sign of shared distress. Throwing up dust they darken the air to symbolise their sorrow (Job 2:12). Thus they enter his misery with a courteous, sensitive and respectful compassion. They try to grasp the extent of his devastation, and for a full week the three sit in silence with Job (v13).

Often we find that the 'way out' promised by God for people oppressed by difficulties (1 Corinthians 10:13) comes by means of other human beings. God sends the gospel to us through the efforts of other people who often pay a high price in terms of time and personal convenience. Still, what a slow business it seems – so few people giving so much to try to reach so many others. Presumably God could as easily transmit his messages straight into our brains without reference to another living soul. Instead he has given us the incarnation as our model: 'As the Father has sent me, I am sending you' (John 20:21). The message in word, act and sign is an embodied message – lived by human beings for the benefit of other human beings.

In Jesus God came to us personally as one of us, totally identifying with us, making himself nothing and taking on the nature of a servant (see Philippians 2:5–11). No remote 'zapping' of prospective converts here, no long-range power play to knock people off their feet and into the kingdom. Rather, 'your king comes to you, gentle . . .' (Matthew 21:5). And Jesus spent an awful amount of time with a handful of people. (See, for example, John 1:35–51 where one disciple tells another about him and gradually, slowly, individuals circle around him before coming close.)

Mass communication is, of course, important to world evangelism. 'Timely technology for the timeless truth' is a gift from God. Yet the fundamental principle of the incarnation remains: *you* are the salt and light of the world, *you* embody the message.

> We loved you so much that we were delighted to share with you not only the gospel of God but our lives as well . . .
>
> *1 Thessalonians 2:8*

THE LAMENT

Job 3

A good man has had enough. Here is the death-wish as seen nowhere else in scripture. Job's words are not a considered reflection on the 'problems of suffering' but a direct response to the impact of the suffering itself. (We know how difficult it is to have holy thoughts while enduring a bout of severe toothache!) He longs for the peace and quiet of Sheol, the ghostly 'waiting-room' in the underworld where the dead gather. Old Testament people dreaded Sheol (see Psalm 88:10–12), but Job cannot wait to escape to its oblivion (Job 3:13–19).

The fear behind his misery is the unthinkable idea that God has, for some inexplicable reason, turned against him (v23). It is not suffering which has become such a problem to Job but God. Even Sheol appears more desirable than this nightmare scenario, for there seems little point in a life which is dying inch by miserable inch (vv20,25,26).

Illness, depression, grief and a sense of being spiritually cast adrift can, we well know, induce a bleak vision. But we expect something better than that from Job, the strong believer of the first two chapters.

He is changing. He is learning. He is travelling. And his lament is part of the process. God stays quiet and allows his man the freedom to grieve. Job's life is desolate and he is allowed to tell God so. Like the prophets and the psalmists, like Jesus on the cross (see Psalm 22; Mark 15:34), he cries out. In scripture and in the traditional worship of the church, the lament is an integral part of prayer. Often when left to our own devices we shape our public worship in an optimistic, upbeat, sunny style. But at a price. What are the people in the congregation who are going through Job-like experiences to do with their pain and their sense of despair?

Lament is more than undisciplined moaning. Every hard knock puts a question mark against the believer's entire relationship with God. It raises the awful possibility of a real abandonment by God. This is enough to terrify the faithful believer whose basis for living assumes God's unbreakable covenant love. 'I have no peace, no quietness; I have no rest, but only turmoil' (Job 3:26). If that is your experience, then tell God so. Lament is prayer without pretending. We are not 'letting the side down' if we voice our anguish to God. Job's experience of life is that it can be a messy, stupefying, terrifying business, and he will not pretend otherwise.

Everything that touches us matters to God. This is the reasoning behind the lament-prayer in scripture. The darkest experiences are considered proper subjects for conversation with God. When Job articulates his hurt and confusion, he is bringing *everything* into God's domain. Nothing in his life is out of bounds to God; there is no pretence. The alternative to behaving like Job is for us to split our inner life into the 'sunny, happy, positive, praiseworthy' stuff which we think we ought to pray and the chaotic, painful stuff which we mutter to ourselves in the dark. But the lament, says Walter Brueggemann, can evoke reality for someone who has engaged in self-deception and still imagines that life is well-ordered when in fact it is not. He calls laments like Job's 'statements of disorientation':[1]

> . . . the harsh and abrasive speech of a statement of disorientation may penetrate the deception and say, 'No, *this* is how it really is.' In such a case *language leads experience* so that the speaker speaks what is unknown and unexperienced until it is finally

brought to speech. It is not this way until it is said to be this way.

It is no wonder that the church has intuitively avoided these psalms [of lament]. They lead us into dangerous acknowledgement of how life really is. They lead us into the presence of God where everything is not polite and civil. They cause us to think unthinkable thoughts and utter unutterable words. Perhaps worst, they lead us away from the comfortable religious claims of *modernity* in which everything is managed and controlled. In our modern experience, but probably also in every successful and affluent culture, it is believed that enough power and knowledge can tame the terror and eliminate the darkness. Very much a 'religion of orientation' operates on that basis. But our honest experience, both personal and public, attests to the resilience of the darkness in spite of us. The remarkable thing about Israel is that it did not banish or deny darkness from its religious enterprise. It embraces the darkness as the very stuff of new life. Indeed, Israel seems to know that new life comes nowhere else.

Integrity will insist that we acknowledge the reality and the tenacity of the darkness that infiltrates our experiences. Faith takes hold of it all and places it under God's sway. For nothing, not even evil and darkness, can exist outside of his control.

We have divine permission to stand in God's presence with our heart-break, but we are not left lamenting. Job has begun his journey towards a vision of God which will be deep, wide and high enough to cover life as it really is (42:1–6). Like Job, we must travel before we arrive at that healing vision for ourselves. Through darkness into light, through death into resurrection, through disorientation into a new orientation – many times over.

God of mystery and revelation, at the extremes of our distress and despair, when you are the only hope left, let us hear your name again, and so take courage on the journey.

I Am Who I Am.
I Shall Be Who I Shall Be,
That Which I Am I Shall Be,
That Which I Shall Be I Am.[2]

AS SPARKS FLY UPWARD

Job 4, 5

Eliphaz responds to Job's outburst with a mixture of real gentleness (Job 4:1–6), encouragement and forthrightness. He avoids trivialising his friend's unhappiness with off-the-shelf platitudes. In a dream, in an awe-inspiring moment, the Spirit draws aside the curtain so that Eliphaz can glimpse the unseen, and he awakes with a message for Job (4:12–16). He throws him three life-belts.

1 Remember God's majestic freedom

No human being is a match for the almighty power of God (4:7–21) who controls human life and nature (5:9–16). Job's passionate resentment (4:2; 5:2) is totally out of place. It is not fate that he is raging against but the omnipotent will of God. Calm down, Job, and submit to whatever God has in mind for you. Trust in the justice and goodness of the One who rules the universe, you 'who are crushed more readily than a moth' (4:19).

2 Allow for the way the world is

'Man is born to trouble as surely as sparks fly upward' (5:7): this principle colours our existence.

We inhabit a wonderful but risky world. 'God makes the world make itself,' said Austin Farrer.[1] He has created a complex physical reality organised on many planes, each interacting with the others, to run the world. The result is this beautiful, stunning creation with its astonishing variety and vitality. But we have it this way at a price. Within this way of 'making the world make itself' there will be accidents, collisions, breaks, malformations, disasters, decline and degeneration as well as power, growth and incredible loveliness.

How does God relate to this teeming order? By 'upholding the universe by the word of his power' (Hebrews 1:2–4; Colossians 1:15–18). Perhaps the most helpful word we can use is 'persuade'. God allows creation (at every level) to be true to itself; but over all and through all he 'persuades' the whole system away from chaos and towards order and pattern.

Pain is an essential factor in the defence, healing and growth of the body. A body which is not sensitive to pain would not survive long. Our pain sensors are the 'burglar alarm' system that warns of intruders. I once met a leprosy sufferer in Thailand, who had lost part of his foot when he stepped back into a fire. The leprosy had deadened his sensitivity to pain. Pain is an unavoidable 'upward-flying spark'.

Another spark is the eco-system of the world. Did an earthquake or a volcanic eruption destroy Job's property (Job 1:16), a tornado collapse the house on his children (1:18–19)? People living in the city of Kobe, Japan, or along the Northridge fault of Los Angeles, who have suffered the terrible effects of earthquake devastation, could sympathise. Earthquakes are a potential hazard for anyone living on a geological fault-line, just as tidal waves and flood devastation can be expected in the Bay of Bengal.

There is nothing 'spiritual' or demonic, or divine, about these phenomena which can be disconcertingly impartial about where they strike. In the recent Alabama tornadoes a church filled with worshippers was flattened. I remember a storm over Cambridge when lightning struck only one building in Mill Road – it knocked the cross off the top of our church, St Barnabas! This is the way the world is; embrace it with courage.

God makes the processes under the earth's mantle make themselves, by natural laws which may result in earth-quakes and volcanoes. Can the processes 'down there' serve us 'up here'? Of course. They keep the earth's temperature about right (too hot, the ice-caps melt and we drown – too cold and we freeze over). Given the way the earth's thermostat works, earthquakes are inevitable. Imagine the chaos should an archangel interfere with the eco-system, cancelling this earthquake and turning down the flame under that volcano! We would be living in an Alice-in-Wonderland world, not our own.

We must add that Almighty God in his majestic freedom is neither locked out of, or locked into, his creation. He 'sustains all things by his powerful word.' He has the power to interfere in creation if he wishes (John 2:1–10).

We are born to trouble because of sin and our sinfulness (Romans 8:19–23). From early on the Bible speaks of damaged personal relations, estrangement between man and woman, and the brutalising of sexual love (Genesis 3:7, 16). We see emerging a society with familiar traits, one that is driven by mistrust and exploitation and which plunges into violent, jealous murder (Genesis 4:1–12). Indeed, much of Job's misery is caused by the greed and brutality of his fellow human beings (Job 1:13–15,17).

In a few words, *Genesis* sketches a discordant spiritual realm where human beings are trapped in self-contradic-tion. On the one hand, they are in flight from God (Genesis 3:8,24); at the same time, they are engaged in struggling against the threat of evil (3:15). On the physical plane, disorder is pictured as a frustrating and painful attempt to sustain and renew the basic processes of life (3:16,19).

Discord is rooted in our collective anarchy against the rule of God. It is an orientation away from the light, which leaves individuals and society vulnerable to the demonic manipulation of man's dreadful hostility to God. We are, all of us, born to (this) trouble and quite unable to reach and exorcise our own sinwardness.

3 Accept adversity as God's discipline

Pin your hopes, Job, on the fact that you have been a 'pious and blameless man' (Job 4:6). Whenever did God allow good people to be destroyed? The only explanation for your sufferings is that it is God's way of training and correcting you. So be glad about it, he is on your side and means you only good (5:19–26, 'You will . . .'). Discipline goes with discipleship. This principle is fundamental to the way we interpret our testing times. Eliphaz is quite right: discipline is precious evidence that our loving, heavenly Father is determined to make something of us (Proverbs 3:11,12; Hebrews 12:4–13). Indeed, be concerned when his shaping, directing influences are *not* working strongly in your life (Hebrews 12:8).

In practice, however, the question arises as to how much adversity a person can take before the experience changes from a constructive to a destructive one? It does look as if Job has crossed the line. C S Lewis strongly advocated the 'megaphone' school of suffering which sees adversity as God's call to us to repent and be changed. His friend, the great theologian Austin Farrer, thought Lewis went too far:[2]

> Man, to Lewis, is an immortal subject; pains are his moral remedies, salutary disciplines, willing sacrifices, playing their part in a dramatic interchange between God and him. But this is not all the truth, nor perhaps half of it. Pain is the sting of death, the foretaste and ultimately the experience of sheer destruction. Pain cannot be related to the will of God as an evil wholly turned into a moral instrument. Pain is the bitter savour of that mortality out of which it is the unimaginable mercy of God to rescue us. When under suffering we see good men go to pieces we do not witness the failure of a moral discipline to take effect; we

witness the advance of death where death comes by inches.

Farrer's comment is a timely reminder to us as we are drawn deeper and deeper into Job's quest. God is not running an impersonal experiment in holiness when he mysteriously works through adversity. Always he is the father with his children, not the laboratory worker with his white mice.

Eliphaz has worked hard for his friend. With traditional, orthodox wisdom (Job 5:27) he has constructed a bridge for Job to cross over from resentment to humble submission. And surely much of what he says speaks into our own situations. However, Job's personal experiences have exposed, for him, the inadequacies of traditional interpretations. He cannot trust the bridge to take him over his troubled waters. He is now more like a fugitive leaping from boat to boat across a river crammed with boats, all moving in opposite directions!

MORE DEEPLY AND MORE TERRIBLY

Job 6, 7

God is Job's problem, not suffering. In his self-pitying, God-blaming mood he holds God responsible for his anguish: for laying this crushing weight of trouble on him (Job 6:2,3), hunting him down for the kill (v4), starving him of mercy and justice so that he cries out like an animal (v5). His pitiful existence is no more rewarding than eating nauseating food (vv6,7). Death would be a merciful release, fulfilling (note the heavy sarcasm) 'the words of the Holy One' (v10). These are terrible things to say, but something fascinating is emerging out of Job's rage:

> What was really new was that Job involved God, in a quite different way, much more deeply and more terribly, in the suffering . . . Job envisages a God who quite personally and with all his powers enters into the suffering and becomes involved in it. That is the only thing he really knows and, indeed, it nearly drives him out of his mind.
>
> *Gerhard von Rad*[1]

Job seems to know intuitively that, whatever the 'answer' to his trouble, it will involve God on the inside with him. He will not allow the Lord to remain on the outside looking in. In this strange tension Job can only turn to the One he blames for his troubles. As Augustine puts it, he takes flight to the One from whom he is in flight like Jacob who clings to the God who wounded him (Genesis 32:22–30).

Ah my deare angrie Lord,
Since thou dost love, yet strike;
Cast down, yet help afford;
Sure I will do the like.
I will complain, yet praise;
I will bewail, approve:
And all my sowre-sweet dayes
I will lament, and love.

George Herbert[2]

Job is still a long way from Herbert's serene resolution but he is moving in that direction. His intuition anticipates the glory of the incarnation, God on the inside with us. In Jesus, God gathered his insider-knowledge of us and curtailed his almighty power so that he could feel and taste this human nature of ours in the heat, and joy, and messiness, and pain of lived experience (Hebrews 2:10–18). He has done the apprenticeship and has come through it qualified to save his people, as one of us.

There are other awesome clues to the insider-God. His disciples identified Jesus after his resurrection by his death marks (John 20:19–31). Those scars, which he carries forever in his resurrection body, are the evidence that he has visited the centre of our existence, has penetrated to the depths of what it means to be human and is committed to life on the inside with us. Job is feeling his way towards this astonishing truth.

Some of Israel's prophets came to the same realisation as they interpreted the nation's Job-like experience in captivity, culminating in Isaiah's Suffering Servant of the Lord (Isaiah 52:13 – 53:12). But no one in Israel had ever described God's activity with people as Job does.

Insiders and outsiders

Suffering separates people around us into 'insiders' and 'outsiders'. Society has an elaborate system of signs to show who are the 'insiders'. For people who have been together through a crisis, there are medals, black arm-bands, badges, reunion events. Now terribly adrift in his isolation, Job lambasts his friends and family (Job 6:14–30). They, poor people, are unable to make sense of his claims and resentments. He accuses them of not making the effort of imagination and fellow-feeling to understand his anguish. He is profoundly disappointed with their inconstancy ('intermittent streams', v15).

Altered perspectives

Job is on the move. His friends are not. New experiences alter our perspectives – if we allow them to. We may be so fixed in our attitudes that we are impervious to the insights of new experiences. As a bouncing tennis ball makes no impression on a nuclear air-raid shelter, so new messages may have no impression on us. Indeed, we may even make a virtue out of our orthodoxy. There is little doubt that Job's friends, for all their concern, showed such tendencies. But people who want to be open to God, and open to his world, must stay alert and agile, ready to make the shift in perspective.

Standing outside St Paul's Cathedral in the centre of London I can see that the dome is convex. When I change my position and go inside I see the dome is also concave. Shifting my perspective gives me a greater understanding of the building.

Hard knocks are opening Job up to a new understanding of reality. With his friends he stands within the wisdom tradition which observed life closely and formulated its conclusions in proverbs and other wisdom literature. Central to the moral scheme of this tradition, was the maxim that people reap what they sow. Good people prosper, bad people suffer. So, if a person is not prospering, it can only suggest there is something wrong in his or her life. There exists an unbreakable correspondence of act and consequence. This is the view held by Job's friends and they are unable to shift their perspective.

However, Job himself has moved on from that position. The old wisdom does not adequately cover the hard facts of life. Yes, sin does produce suffering in some form or other. But it does not follow that *all* suffering is the result of sin. Job's experiences have altered his perspective.

'You are such a fast God and always leaving just as we arrive,' said R S Thomas. Why is that? In order to move us on, shift our location, break up the old mind-set, so that we can know more of the love of Christ 'that suppasses knowledge' (Ephesians 3:19). In that sense we can share in John Donne's exuberant celebration of travelling on – 'Change is the nursery of music, joy, life and eternity' – although it may not always seem like it at the time.

No one in their right mind would choose to go through some of these perspective-changing experiences. Yet (and how often this is the case – just ask around) in retrospect, and sometimes only years later, those events appear to us as golden times – life-changing times we call them because then, desperate and naked, we were thrown upon God. The knocks, the shocks, the experiences, the changes, the altered perspectives are God's means of unshuttering our minds to let in the revelation which is already at the door.

Most people have memories of such experiences. I recall a time of great disorientation when, after some years of missionary work in Thailand (which we vastly enjoyed and believed to be the will of God) our family's health fell apart. We were back home before we knew it. The ill health was difficult enough, but the whole thing was made nightmarish by its apparent senselessness and the seeming absence (or indifference) of God. Over several years the experience changed me profoundly. My pre-crisis view of God was simply too neat and superficial to cope with this new reality. My perspectives changed. It was a life-changing, God-finding time and continues to be so.

People not programmes

Now we can see that Job *will* come through to wisdom and serenity in the end (Job 42:5). If it was merely a matter of finding answers to problems about suffering or supplying data about 'the will of God' then, no doubt, a few memos from heaven would do it. But *people* are God's plan. Job is his plan. God is working with *human beings*, not programmes and blueprints. Divine providence is not about supplying answers to conundrums, but transforming men and women as love and holiness are worked into the texture of their lives.

As he engages with God who is on the inside with him, and as he goes through much anguish, Job is becoming another person, someone who is, in the biblical metaphor of 'the white stone', called by 'a new name ... known only to him who receives it' (Revelation 2:17). Only that person can read the name and understand it because he has become that name.

WE ARE MERE YESTERDAYS

Job 8

It is Bildad's guess that suffering has unhinged Job's mind. Why else would someone reared in the old certainties storm against God so outrageously? Bildad fires two warning shots across Job's bows.

Beware amnesia!

Job talks like a man who has forgotten his roots in the wisdom tradition of 'the former generations ... and ... their fathers' (Job 8:8–10). However, the individual is short-lived and very limited in his experience – we are mere yesterdays (v9) – and ought to show a certain humility in the presence of the 'fathers'. Even though their view of suffering-as-retribution is one-eyed (vv3–6,20), that limitation does not invalidate the riches of their spirituality streaming down to us out of Israel's past.

Beware amnesia! Bildad's rebuke to Job is, if anything, even more appropriate for us in our culture of high-speed forgetting. Just try to buy a copy of yesterday's newspaper! Amnesia, a deep forgetting, scuttles the past and we act as if only the present has any claims on us. Those of us living in the developed world overrate the present and take it far too seriously (the-latest-is-the-greatest) as if wisdom arrived with our generation (v10). But 'we are mere yesterdays'.

Thus self-realisation, not God's law, becomes the standard for moral judgement and any appeals to tradition or transcendent order are scuppered by our inability to look upward, backward or outward. We look in the only direction left to us, which is inward. How *we* feel about something overrules what *God* has said about it. So beware amnesia!

Bildad wants to reconnect Job to his roots. How far back is he going when he refers to 'former generations' (v8)? Isaiah is much more specific when he also warns against memory loss: 'Look to the rock from which you were cut... look to Abraham... and to Sarah' (Isaiah 51:1,2). Israel in Babylonian captivity was in danger of forgetting her origins. Living among their successful and powerful captors, we can imagine how the Israelites would stress the more impressive and respectable aspects of their history, like Solomon's Temple and the monarchy. Yet Isaiah calls them back beyond the flattering, socially acceptable memories to the primitive events in the lives of Abraham and Sarah.

Israel, remember Abraham, your father, famous for his faith (see Romans 4:16–25). Yes, but remember the full story about him, not only the splendid bits. Get back to him in his bewilderment, shielding behind Sarah's skirts, lying to save his skin (Genesis 12:10–20), trusting God for a son one moment and the next taking a surrogate wife just for insurance. And get back to Sarah. She did, in the end, laugh her Easter laughter at the gift of a son, but remember the full story about her too, her barrenness, her old age, her cynical laughter at God's offer of a child, her inability to receive God's promised future (Genesis 18:10–15). We are born out of that Sarah.

In Abraham and Sarah God worked his miracle, an awesome inversion of the facts; against all reason, he overwhelmed their impotence with the gift of Isaac. And he promised Sarah (and through Sarah to us) that she would have many descendants (see Isaiah 54:1–3).

The point of this remembering is to bring us back to the 'DNA' of our faith. Our spiritual origins are not in sophisticated, clever, philosophical explorations but in God's gift of resurrection to our death. This recovery of solidarity with Abraham and Sarah is what prepares exiles for restoration (Isaiah 52:11,12). Abraham and Sarah cast themselves on God with a primitive and desperate dependence. Their story models our own urgent self-abandonment to the God of life-out-of-death. The story is the lens through which we perceive the world as the place where the power of God works, in spite of our inability to explain it or initiate it any more than death can explain or initiate resurrection.

Fragile life, hanging by a thread

Once we allow 'the former generations' to speak to us, our modern complacency is demolished. They tell us things which are near-blasphemous to the prevailing secularism with its myth of autonomous self-sufficiency. They describe the precarious fragility of our fleeting, unstable existence (Job 8:11,12) like swinging on a spider's web (vv14,15). We long for permanence, to be known, appreciated, reckoned significant, remembered among our own people. Instead we are transient hostel-dwellers, rootless, leaving no trace of a presence, superseded by the stream of succeeding generations (vv16–19). The most heart-rending aspect of our existence is that the world's mysterious beauty is fragile and fugitive. We experience its elusiveness as a real nostalgia, a joy out of our reach, even when we do manage to escape our claustrophobic secularism.

> As if the sea should part
> And show a further sea –
> And that – a further – and the three
> But a presumption be –
>
> Of periods of seas –
> Unvisited of shores –
> Themselves the verge of seas to be –
> Eternity – is those.

Emily Dickinson[1]

Bildad's point is that, faced with the mystery of our life in God's world, we do well to submit to him in humility and obedience (vv20–22). It is arrogant to imagine we could work our way out of mystery and into clarity. For, says a writer, 'the true alternative is not mystery or clarity, but mystery or absurdity.'

We can be grateful to Bildad and the 'former generations' for calling us to our senses, especially those of us who are children of a know-all, control-all and possess-all culture which looks upon unresolved mystery as a failure.

And yet . . .

Something about Bildad is not quite right. His tone is worrying: it is too harsh and cocksure. Fixed on his doctrine of retribution, he places the worst interpretation on the death of Job's children (v4). There is no indication that he has heard Job's argument that, while all sin does indeed disrupt, not all disruption is due to sin. In fact, Bildad sounds like a man in real danger of shielding himself from life by hiding behind theories about life. We see similar attitudes in a certain kind of institutionalised religion: law instead of grace, dogma instead of life, no generosity of spirit but defensiveness, rigid codes and petrified moralities.

This attitude saves Bildad the hard work of opening up to Job as a fellow member of the human family; he treats him as though he were a remote, card-carrying theologian. It was different with our Lord Jesus. He allowed no theologizing about the causes of a man's blindness; that poor man had our Lord's immediate and personal practical help (John 9:1–7).

STEPPING-STONES

Job 9, 10

By now it is clear why Job has his special place in the folklore of the human family. Someone must express our bewilderment at what God actually does for the world when measured against what we feel he *could* do. This spokesperson needs to be an 'insider,' not an enemy of God, a person with the knowingness of a believer and a lover. Job stands in solidarity with all who are tempted to grow bitter at the way God's power enacts God's justice. To summarise this enigma, 'If God is God, he is not good; if God is good, he is not God'.

Eliphaz may extol the kindly power of God (Job 5:9–16): 'So the poor have hope, and injustice shuts its mouth' (v16). Bildad can ask incredulously, 'Does God pervert justice?' (8:3). But Job has been robbed and they have not. Just as they did not recognise him physically (2:12), so they fail to understand him emotionally. Their general principles for the moral ordering of life strike Job as theoretical. General principles are for 'mankind' but Job is not mankind, he is one particular case, and he will not cower before his friends' shining confidence.

> Of course – I prayed –
> And did God care?
> He cared as much as on the Air
> A bird – had stamped her foot –
> And cried 'Give me' –
> My reason – life –
> I had not had – but for yourself –

> 'Twere better charity
> To leave me in the Atom's tomb –
> Merry, and Nought, and gay, and numb –
> Than this smart misery.
>
> *Emily Dickinson*[1] (see Job 10:18–22)

His friends' statements drive Job to the opposite extreme of dark despair so that he can now see only a sinister side to their position. Divine power and might are violent and destructive (9:1–9). And where is justice with a God so terribly elusive (9:11) and so unwilling to state his complaint against Job 'in court' (9:14–21; 10:2)?

This God, as Job now perceives him, is like a reckless and unpredictable driver in charge of a cosmic steamroller, who makes up his own highway code as he proceeds (vv13–35). The plane falling out of the sky, the fire raging through the tower block, the slaughter in an African tribal war: 'It is all the same; that is why I say, "He destroys both the blameless and the wicked" ' (v22).

Yet Job is also aware of God's close interest in his affairs – as a mouse is aware of a cat: probing (10:6,7), hounding (v16), overwhelming (v17), gazing. He longs for respite from God's stare (vv14,20). Israel may celebrate her sense of security within the light of the divine countenance (Numbers 6:22–27) but Job feels the eyes of the implacable hunter upon him: 'Turn away from me so that I can have a moment's joy' (Job 10:20). This is as bleak as it gets for Job. Again, we notice that God remains silent during these ferocious attacks. He allows Job to make an essential journey out of his false perception of divine providence towards the truth. There are three stepping-stones to support him.

1 Hanging on

Given the chaos in the man we marvel at Job's stability. For all his raging at God, is he is least, raging *at God*, facing towards God. He still believes that any answers to his dilemma will be found in God and not elsewhere: 'Lord, to whom shall we go? You have the words of eternal life' (John 6:68). He sticks it out. It is a patience that allows the inscrutable processes of divine love to work within his experiences.

2 God the personal creator

In Job 10:3,8–11,18 we have the exquisite pictures of the Artist-Creator who shapes Job like a potter (vv8,9), and metaphors of cheese-making (v10) and knitting (v11) for the processes of conception and growth in the womb. God personally supervises the individual's creation with painstaking attention to detail (*cf* Psalm 139:13). The imagery recalls G K Chesterton's idea that 'to every person that ever lived had been given a definite and unique confidence of God. Each one of us is engaged on secret service; each one of us has a peculiar message . . . of which our thoughts, our faces, our bodies, our hats, our boots, our tastes, our virtues, and even our vices, are more or less fragmentary and inadequate expressions'.[2]

Does it make sense, therefore, to believe that the God who created Job thus would then destroy him? Job's warm and tender feelings towards God as his personal Creator at this moment are the first signs that he is open to other thoughts: there is, after all, more to God than power and might. A literal translation of Job 10:13 runs 'But these things [the marks of your concern] you have hidden in your heart, I know that it [your love] was within you'. This is not to claim 'a rational world-order which can be made clear to everyone, but a direct confrontation with the pressure of the miraculous and mysterious God, to whose hidden abysses suffering, too, belongs' (Eichrodt).[3]

3 The go-between

Is there an impartial arbiter who will hold the scales evenly between Job and his cosmic opponent (9:32–35)? This wistful plea for a just go-between, a mediator, occurs twice again (16:19; 19:25), and each time the context is one of black despair. Each time there emerges the fundamental truth that God himself will provide a go-between for God and man; again we come to this truth about 'fleeing from God to God'.

> When all within is dark,
> And thy just angers rise,
> From thee I turn to thee,
> And find love in thine eyes.
>
> *Immanuel of Rome*[4]

The name of that love is Jesus, the mediator between God and man (1 Timothy 2:3–6). Not, thank God, an impersonal, uninvolved arbiter only, but our true, representative Man who is in solidarity with his troubled people and undertakes to bring us to God, for he is God. He is the place of meeting between God and humankind since both natures meet in him.

Three stepping-stones which can start Job on his walk towards the light. They are solid ground under the feet of all who need to make that journey.

BEYOND THE WORM'S-EYE VIEW

Job 11

It is not difficult to dislike Zophar. He sounds a bit of a bully determined to knock some sense into poor Job. One writer so objects to Zophar's attitude (Job 11:1–6,12) that he believes 'there must be a special place in hell for those who are clever enough with words to use God to humiliate men' (John Gibson).[1] An 'ivory-tower' theologian who fails to engage with real life, a man who filters Job's experiences through his own limited theories, Zophar is not the most attractive of the friends. Yet there is more to him. Surely it is good that in this man Job has a friend who will not allow himself to be drawn into the morass of his self-pity. We need our no-nonsense friends to stand up to us and, when necessary, to speak a few home truths.

Zophar also follows the predictable line of suffering-as-retribution (vv10–12) and blessing-as-reward (vv13–20). Yet he does have at least one interesting message to make us sit up and take notice. The way he delivers it is about as subtle as a brass band, but then his purpose is to knock a hole in Job's stubborn pessimism. His message is this: 'true wisdom has two sides' (v6).

Can you possibly know what you are doing, Job, when you accuse God of injustice? God is beyond our grasp (v6,7). 'Can you fathom the mysteries of God?' We cannot even begin to think about him except in earth-bound terms which imitate something of his being. His immensity, his hiddenness, his uniqueness we can only hint at by extremes of height and depth, astronomical and invisible (vv8,9). God is . . . himself. For a mere man to come lecturing the

Almighty is evidence that he is a hollow, empty individual (witless, v12), as stubbornly stupid as a wild donkey.

There is a lovely story about Augustine walking along a beach immersed in thought, trying to 'probe the limits of the Almighty' (v7). He sees a boy (an angel) playing in the surf, scooping water onto the beach with a spoon while laughing and pointing at Augustine. In his own way Zophar attempts to teach Job the same lesson, mocking the arrogance of the man who is trying to 'empty the ocean' of divine mysteries with the 'small spoon' of his intellect.

Yet God is the most glorious subject for our minds. 'Great are the works of the Lord; they are pondered by all who delight in them' (Psalm 111:2). In this attitude of adoration, curiosity is the beginning of wisdom for us. And, says Zophar, 'True wisdom has two sides' – a term which means that it is manifold, too deep for our comprehension, so that we are unable to fathom it. Zophar's point is that Job should not mistake his limited insights into wisdom and truth for the whole story.

Christians can go much further, of course, since 'Christ Jesus . . . has become for us wisdom from God' (1 Corinthians 1:30). Not that we can get our minds around that truth any more easily. Rather the opposite, for the paradox of eternal wisdom, come to us in the Child born to Mary two thousand years ago, is even more utterly stunning: 'immensity cloistered in thy dear womb' (Donne). Nevertheless the incarnation does mean that our relationship to truth and wisdom is now relationship with a person, Jesus of Nazareth, and not with abstract speculations: 'Christ, in whom are hidden all the treasures of wisdom and knowledge' (Colossians 2:3).

We are each of us at various stages of discovering the depths of the riches of God in Christ Jesus. The journey will bring us face to face with God (Revelation 22:4) which will be the beginning of heaven for us. In the present journey, what I must not do is to expect that everything will fall within my 'worm's-eye view', because it does not and it cannot. My own tiny discoveries need to be complemented by those diverse and vivid discoveries experienced by God's people throughout the world and throughout time.

This mutual encouragement of one another into fresh reali-sations of the wisdom and love of God may be compared to music-making.[2] The members of an orchestra gather for a performance. Their instruments and musical skills are strikingly different – the orchestra requires the fullest pos-sible range of sounds so that it can perfectly express the music which sings in the composer's imagination and which is now written in the score lying open on the con-ductor's stand. The players tune up. Each one is concerned with himself and his own instrument, playing to himself. The noise is awful! At this moment the audience cannot see the reason for this particular combination of instru-ments or why this one is placed next to that one. But when the conductor enters and lifts his baton the cacophony is transformed into beautiful symphony.

Creation is like a great orchestra. God is the composer. His interpreter and conductor is Jesus Christ the Son of God, 'the heir of all things' (Hebrews 1:2). He knows perfectly the Composer's mind and at the same time is personally involved with the development of the orchestra. In fact in this analogy there is no audience, unless it is God himself. Everything in creation is a performer. This is the reason for creation's existence. It is in the act of playing that 'all things' can discover why they have been called together into this orchestra.

Bringing these thoughts to bear on Zophar's insights – that we should go humbly into the wisdom of God which transcends the grasp of any one person – our orchestral analogy tells us that we should delight in the astonishing diversity of wisdom experienced among the people of God. The Conductor requires the greatest possible range if he is to offer beautiful music to the Father; therefore we must generously encourage each other as we pursue afresh the wisdom of God. Your discoveries are not a criticism or a contradiction of my own, although they may very well be a challenge to me. The lemming-like uniformity which seems to plague our church life derives, in part at least, from insecurity and fear when confronted by Christians who are breaking new ground as they track the wisdom of God. (We are seeing this today particularly in the realm of Mission). Plurality is essential for symphony, Christ's symphony, in which our lives are drawn up into a transcendent unity under his discipline and inspiration. We relate to him and to each other symphonically.

You will have felt the irony in all of this. Here Zophar lectures Job on the need to allow many instruments to play their various parts in the symphony of God's wisdom. Yet in fact Job throughout his story is pleading with his friends to acknowledge this very thing! I suspect that the difference between the two men is something like this: Zophar recognises mentally the manifold nature of the wisdom of God. Job is prepared to pay the price of being misunderstood and misrepresented as he allows the wisdom of God to change him.

LET GOD BE GOD

Job 12 – 14

By this time Job is more than a shade paranoid! Still, there is something magnificent and moving in his third response to his friends. In spite of his fierce row with God, he still fights for God's good name.

Defending God from God's defenders

Job has listened to his friends and decides they are committing the sin of patronising God with their flattery. Take the 'glossy brochure pictures' of the good life in the speeches of Eliphaz and Zophar (Job 5:17–27; 11:13–20). Why do these two feel they must talk-up their faith like this? God's self-appointed public relations men, they wrap him in the cotton wool of their highly selective accounts of divine providence, smoothing the jagged edges of his mysterious ways with his world. Perhaps they doubt God's ability to defend himself in the eyes of a world critical of his control. Or perhaps their desire to paint the picture in softer, kinder colours is a symptom of their own spiritual insecurities.

Job will have none of it. He calls the friends 'plasterers of lies' (13:4) who cover over the realities of divine providence and imagine they are thereby defending God's reputation. But in fact they 'speak wickedly on God's behalf . . . speak deceitfully for him . . . show him partiality' (13:7–10). Their misguided efforts are 'ashes' and 'clay' (v12) which will bring down God's 'splendour' and 'dread' upon their heads (v11).

There is a striking saying in the Talmud: 'The prophets

know that their God is a God of truth who cannot be flattered'. For all his anger Job stands within the spirit of that saying. His disagreements with God are far more God-honouring than his friends' flatteries. He refuses to tinker with the truth, however awkward it is (13:1). He will be honest, a quality that is itself a measure of the deepest faith in God. Therefore (and Job is always the extremist) he counteracts his friends' idealised and glowing accounts by stressing divine power negatively as seen in natural devastation (12:15), and in national and international disruption (vv16–25). He is determined to be God's true witness, not his smooth-talking salesman.

> Extol thee – could I? Then I will
> By saying nothing new –
> But just the truest truth
> That thou art heavenly.
>
> Perceiving thee is evidence
> That we are of the sky–
> Partaking thee a guaranty
> Of immortality.
>
> *Emily Dickinson*[1]

Complete honesty requires a faith grounded in the conviction that the justice and wisdom of God are at work in human affairs. Only then dare we embrace God's hard saying:

> I form the light and create darkness,
> > I bring prosperity and create disaster;
> > I, the Lord, do all these things.
>
> *Isaiah 45:7*

Light and darkness are both instruments of his will. They are not warring twins, equal and opposite regimes. God is *all* and there is nothing else but *God* (Isaiah 43:10).

Darkness and disaster depend for their existence upon divine permission, just as Hitler could draw breath only by that permission. Yet everything, including darkness and disaster in any form, is subject to the majestic and redeeming control of the statement 'I bring shalom' (translated in the NIV as 'prosperity', Isaiah 45:7) with its root idea of harmony, integration – the opposite to evil, disaster, chaos, fragmentation. Nothing is allowed to escape the transforming power of God's 'shalom-imparting' grasp on the totality of our affairs: 'And we know that in all things God works for the good of those who love him . . .' (Romans 8:28–39).

We go to the cross of Christ for the definitive enactment of that truth. Everything is gathered there, all the powers of evil. There the whole force of the world's sin crashed into Christ's body. He absorbed the full lethal power of the blow. Out of it, in resurrection, God brought his everlasting shalom for mankind and for all creation (Hebrews 9:15,23–28).

But God-flatterers (past or present) grow uneasy with the all-inclusiveness of Isaiah's view which Job has discovered for himself. They fear it will give God a bad name with the public. In all honesty, most of us share their anxieties. We, too, long for God to be popular – a celebrity! We, too, tend to smooth the way for God to enter the Interest Zone of our friends by rendering him more 'user-friendly'. But Jesus teaches that it is the *truth* which will set people free (John 8:32) and we are struck by the fact that he avoided popularity like the plague. We know how little store Jesus set by the crowd's adulation (John 2:23–25). The truth and popular acclaim would seem to be mutually exclusive. People's right to say 'We like you' implies their equal right to say 'We hate you'. If we crave the public's applause for Christ, we invite the possibility of their contempt also. Their praise implies their right to criticise.

The point is this: God-flatterers, however well meaning, will try to portray God in a way that encourages others to feel 'now *that's* the sort of God I could believe in'. However, tampering with the uncomfortable, immense, mysterious, craggy truth of God claims an appalling price. It is like catching a great, flashing, leaping barracuda and reducing it to fish fingers: manageable, marketable, bite-size, uniform, predictable, convenient, certainly practical – and very, very dead.

Real believers, like Job, choose to go with the undiminished mystery of God. 'We praise you for your glory'. They delight in the fact that they *cannot* explain God and that God has given something far more wonderful than an explanation:

> God does not give us explanations; he gives up a Son. Such is the spirit of the angel's message to the shepherds: 'Peace upon earth, good will to men . . . and this shall be the sign unto you: you shall find a babe wrapped in swaddling clothes, and lying in a manger.'
>
> A Son is better than an explanation. The explanation of our death leaves us no less dead than we were; but a Son gives us a life, in which to live . . . if we live in the Son whom God has given we have a life which will not fail, but always deepen and extend. This is the peace, this is the joy God gives: our joy is swaddled in the cradle, our peace is crucified, our glory rises from the tomb.
>
> *Austin Farrer*[2]

Life in the cul-de-sac

Christ is risen! Yet the fear of death continues to permeate our society. Any minister will tell you how, of all events, the funeral service is unique in the way people attend to what is said. Even for church-goers, the resurrection of Jesus from the dead can be perceived more as a consolation prize than the total reshaping of reality in the risen Christ which it is.

Imagine then, the spiritual world of Job's era. There was nothing to challenge the final joylessness of Sheol (Job 14:14), no certainty of a death-defeating resurrection. Job does indicate a degree of hope from time to time (10:8–12; 13:15; 14:15) but this is quickly quenched. Life is no more than it appears to be: short, brutish, unfair, pointless, 'a wind-blown leaf' (13:25 and 8:14–19). For huge sections of the human family today this is more or less how it continues to be. This view of life, unredeemed by the expectation of a joyful resurrection of the body to eternal life, must bring us to the despair of Job 14, in which the natural renewal of a felled tree (vv7–9) is marvellous compared to a man's cul-de-sac existence (13:28; 14:10).

Before we lose ourselves in the enormous uplift of resurrection faith, we should pause to realise that Job's moving, wistful, sad vision of life is still the norm for vast numbers of people. They struggle on without the light of Christ as the risen Saviour who is 'bringing many sons to glory' (Hebrews 2:10). A tragic condition, which Paul summed up simply as 'without Christ and without hope in the world'.

By the Holy Spirit we receive the seeds of glory in our hearts here and now. They germinate, take root, and reach up towards the light of God's eternity.

Our faith is nonsense without this sense of moving upwards. Heaven must have the supreme place in our total vision if we are to live with freedom and courage in the present. Only heaven can interpret the mystery of our present experiences. It is not merely a prize for walking faithfully with God; it is where the walk takes us. It is the meaning of the walk, 'endless beginning, ceaseless wonder, perpetual resurrection in the inexhausted power of him who everlastingly makes all things new' (Austin Farrer).[3]

Heaven is leading us to itself because there the glory of the Lord dwells. 'God glorifies himself when he shows himself as he is' (Karl Barth). 'That is heaven: God-seen-as-he-is by people transformed and able to delight in the fire of his glorious presence (Revelation 21:1–14).

AT THE TRUE HEART AND CENTRE
OF THINGS

Job 15

How did a man like Eliphaz experience God? How did he expect God to come to him? It is unwise to categorise people too neatly, although Job and his friends were doing just that to each other all the time!

Who would have guessed that Eliphaz, loyal defender of the old school, whose duty was to 'crank the dogma-mill' (Robertson Davies) would have a charismatic experience of revelation that is second to none? We recall that remarkable dream encounter of his, when the Holy Spirit came to him whispering the word of God (Job 4:12–17) an authentic and powerful description of the sensation of inspiration and revelation. He values the experience without falling into our modern errors. For the question invariably follows: why turn from the fire of a first-hand unmediated experience of God to, as it were, a second-hand one, the painstaking reading of his word? Congregations have split over this issue, whole movements evolve around one or other of the two positions – Spirit or word?

Yet Eliphaz and the prophets and seers of the Bible would be puzzled by the distinction. Theirs was a spirituality of word *through* Spirit. Thus Eliphaz also esteemed 'what wise men have declared, hiding nothing received from their fathers (to whom alone the land was given when no alien passed among them)' (15:17–19). But the land was always shared with 'the alien' who was always part of the ethnic mix. This passage cannot refer to a golden time of a pure community of believers; it refers rather to a stream of spirituality as yet uncontaminated by pagan influences.

Therefore people of the Eliphaz school did not simply swallow the old traditions uncritically. They made distinctions. Their purpose was to draw water from the pure, deep well; to get in touch with God through the rich wisdom of his inspired servants of the past and the accumulated experience of the 'fathers'. John Baillie suggests that we find that strong, primitive spirituality, rich in rugged communion with God, in the Psalmists. To take a simple example: 'On my bed I remember you; I think of you through the watches of the night' (Psalm 63:6).

In the materialistic, technological West we have vastly more information and know-how about the world than Job and his friends did in their obscure, backward eastern tribe-lands. 'Flat-earthers', they thought the sun took a dip in the Mediterranean each day at sunset. But compare our night-thoughts with theirs. We go to bed with our minds teeming with the anxieties of the day, or perhaps we turn-in restless with boredom. They, in more basic circumstances, wrapped in flea-ridden blankets – what did they, our 'fathers', think about? We know from their writings:

> At midnight I rise to give you thanks for your
>   righteous laws . . .
> My eyes stay open through the watches of the night,
>   that I may meditate on your promises.
>
> On my bed I remember you; I think of you through
>   the watches of the night.
>
> *Psalms 119:62,148;63:6*

Can we read those words without a sudden sense of humiliation and a collapse of our self-esteem? Where is now our vaunted superiority, our proud boast of belonging to a higher culture? . . . These old worthies went to the centre at once, when they composed themselves to sleep they were thinking upon God's word.

Our modern lives have enough and to spare of diversity in them, but they are sadly lacking in unity. The Psalmists' lives would seem to us lacking in diversity but about their unity there was no doubt. And whenever they had a little time to spare they used it to strengthen that unity. In their own favourite phrase they made certain that however mind and body were occupied their 'heart was fixed'.

John Baillie[1]

Who today would question our urgent need to get back to that deep and pure well?

The link between Spirit and word in the wisdom tradition is made in meditation. No doubt the Sovereign Lord can come to us through any media he chooses, since all creation is transparent to him. But people communicate through language, and the Lord has covenanted to reveal himself – Father and Son – when, in the Holy Spirit, we attend to his words (John 14:23). In meditation (Christian, biblical meditation) we think with the heart, allowing the word of God to call together our scattered inner life. As we turn the words (a verse, a phrase, a picture, a metaphor) over and over in our imagination, words will dissolve into interior prayer. Thus we listen to God's word in meditation and breathe back our response in prayer.

The art of living is contained in this discipline of 'word – meditation – prayer'. Communion with God becomes the pace-maker within us from which all other things take their tempo. As we go about our usual round of duties, work, appointments, leisure, this inner activity goes with us. Do you say this is hopelessly unrealistic within the demands of the real world? Then remember John Baillie's comment that wisdom, as practised by the Psalmists, meant that whenever they had a little time to spare, they used it to strengthen their inner unity. For all our business, most of us actually have more unoccupied spare time than we say. C H Spurgeon compared the 'word – meditation – prayer' process to sucking a throat lozenge. You do not consciously think, 'I am now sucking this sweet.' You just do it and its soothing juices seep down the throat.

Far from triggering a sort of schizophrenic activity, in which we have a part of our mind on God when it ought to be wholly on the work in hand, meditation effects the incomparable healing (shalom) of a unified inner life. Barry Ulanov comments:[2]

> The whole issue of finding time to pray just washes away. We achieve something of what Anthony Bloom calls the holiday spirit of prayer, a sense of celebration in which schedules and time-slots simply fade away.

In practice we discover that the 'word – meditation – prayer' process creates its own climate within us. And we know how certain climates produce, eventually, their characteristic landscapes.

> Our conclusion then must be that while indeed our modern life is adorned with many gifts and graces which the Psalmists lacked, we remain vastly their inferiors until and unless we bring these greater blessings into the same intimate relation to the true heart and centre of things as they brought their most restricted ones . . . only this one thing is absolutely needful.
>
> *John Baillie*[3]

Holy God, loving Father of the Word everlasting,
Grant me to have of thee this living prayer –
Lighten my understanding,

Kindle my will,
Begin my doing,
Incite my love,
Strengthen my weakness,
Enfold my desire.
Amen.

Traditional Scottish Gaelic prayer

WE HAVE A FRIEND

Job 16, 17

The novelist Iris Murdoch wrote something to the effect that 'boring people are those who stop telling the truth'. Job was no bore. He longed for the truth to come out. The poor man on the ash-heap can lead us further and further into God as he hunts for the truth. But he will do it in his own way. His explorations and pronouncements make us distinctly uneasy at times. He has his nightmare: that the God who once poured out his love on him has abandoned him to personal ruin. It is the reversal of all the fundamentals of Job's former life, as if white has become black and yes is now no. All restraint goes. He compares God to a ferocious animal (Job 16:9), a wrestler who pounces on him (vv11,12) and even to a sadistic archer who uses Job for a target (vv12,13). Yet this man speaks things which are half-formed in the back of our own minds and which we hardly dare acknowledge.

The violence of God?

Is God violent, as Job claims (16:7–14)? The Bible does not portray God as a sort of civilised English gentleman, too well-mannered to get into a brawl, essentially nice and dressed by Harrods. Could such a pleasant God really tame the rebellious principalities and powers of spiritual darkness? It was a rough, dirty fight when he defeated his enemies by the shocking violence of the cross. Paul uses gladiatorial language to describe it: 'He forgave us all our sins . . . nailing [them] to the cross. And having disarmed the powers and authorities, he made a public spectacle of them, triumphing over them by the cross' (Colossians 2:13–15). Violent language, and entirely in keeping with Moses' great shout: 'The Lord is a warrior; the Lord is his name. Pharaoh's chariots and his army he has hurled into the sea' (Exodus 15:3–4).

Making every allowance for Job's flourishing persecution-complex, we are still left with a picture of a God who takes a fighter's initiative as he grapples with people and situations. A long way, this, from W H Auden's 'modest Church-of-England God'. If one asked people like Moses, Job, Isaiah (remember 45:7) and John (the book of *Revelation*) where they thought God was in relation to the chaos in the world, their answer would surely be: he is in the thick of it.

Yet the word 'violence', as we commonly use it, cannot be applied to God because it implies strength which is out of control or driven by cruelty. So let us say simply that God can strike as well as caress, that he commands as well as invites, and that he means to do what he does. For it remains true, even at the height of New Testament Christology, that 'we know him who said ... "The Lord will judge his people." It is a dreadful thing to fall into the hands of the living God' (Hebrews 10:30–31). Although Job is prone to use manic imagery, he also expresses our fundamental dilemma in relating to God. Is joyful, confident communion possible with him, Job's strong, all-holy God? Is it not true that the shadow of his anger falls across our conscience whenever we turn to him in prayer? We need a way in.

A friend

From the bleakness of Job's vision there emerges again that mysterious other person whom we first met as the go-between (Job 9:33) and who later will appear as Job's Redeemer (19:25), here described in a wonderful cluster of images as Job's witness, advocate, intercessor, friend (16:19–21). Who is he?

He is God, coming out from God, in solidarity with Job and on his behalf. God-for-me comes out to stand next to me facing God-against-me. My Judge is also my Saviour. It is fascinating to find this principle of 'fleeing from God to God' expressed movingly in post-biblical Judaism:

> Therefore though you slay me, I will trust in you.
> For if you pursue my iniquity
> I will flee from you to yourself
> And I will shelter myself from your wrath in your
>   shadow,
> And to the skirts of your mercies I will lay hold
> Until you have mercy on me
> And I will not let you go till you bless me.
>
> *Solomon Ibn Gabriol*[1]

This is very beautiful, but it still begs the question, 'Who is he who reasons with God, as God, on our behalf?'

Job has seen into the God-head and anticipates the glory of the gospel. Our 'witness, advocate, intercessor, friend' is the second person of the Trinity – Jesus the Son of God. 'We have one who speaks to the Father in our defence – Jesus Christ the Righteous One' (1 John 2:1).

Not only does Jesus speak for us, he is the language that we speak to God – all our communion with the Father is routed through the Son. As Calvin said, we pray through the lips of Jesus, our voices mingle with his voice, our prayer and praise are taken into his prayer and praise where they are cleansed, interpreted and raised to the very highest power in Christ's prayers, *as* Christ's prayers – an acceptable offering. It is the Holy Spirit, poured out upon us by the Father, who connects us to Jesus, our witness, advocate, intercessor, friend. 'Your life is now hidden with Christ in God' (Colossians 3:3).

The wonder of this truth and its practical, saving power is helpfully illustrated by Professor James Torrance.[2] He asks us to imagine going to church on a Sunday morning. There worship (we think) is something that *we* do: we sing hymns; we pray for the world; we listen to the sermon; we offer our money, time and talents to the Lord. Certainly we ask for God's grace to help us do these things, and we have Jesus' example to go by, but worship originates with us.

If that is our attitude, in Job's language, it means we do not feel the desperate need for a 'witness, advocate, intercessor, friend'. The only priesthood at work is *our* priesthood, the only offering is *our* offering, the only intercessions *our* intercessions. James Torrance calls this practice 'unitarian', a kind of do-it-yourself-with-the-help-of-the-minister worship.

Do we seriously believe such worship could ever be worthy of and acceptable to God? Notice the tremendous preoccupation today with mood, atmospherics and especially with group-dynamics, which too often act as the go-between (witness, advocate, intercessor, friend), linking the congregation to God. No wonder we often come away from worship disappointed because 'nothing happened for me' and with the idea that maybe if we sack the music group and get a better one we will 'get through' to God more effectively!

But God does not leave us to our own devices like that: 'it is by grace you have been saved, through faith' (Ephesians 2:8). This holds true for every aspect of our existence, especially for our worship. The truth is that when a church comes together to worship, we gather around the One who is already there, Jesus – our witness, advocate, intercessor, friend – who lives amongst us to bring us to God. 'He is the Proper Man,' said Martin Luther, who stands before the Father offering praise, adoration, intercessions, gifts, as we all should but cannot.

The Holy Spirit streams from the Father through the mind of Christ into his people to inform and inspire their worship. The Spirit then returns through the Son, mingling our imperfect, damaged worship with his perfect worship and raising it up to the Father. Therefore our worship is a *participation* (that is the key word) in Christ's worship (1 Corinthians 2:10–16; Hebrews 7:22–8:3). Through Jesus we 'have access to the Father by one Spirit' (Ephesians 2:18). Whatever physical form it may take, that is the inner dynamic of true ecumenism.

James Torrance refers to Paul's words concerning the Lord's Supper: 'Is not the cup of thanksgiving for which we give thanks a participation in the blood of Christ? And is not the bread that we break a participation in the body of Christ?' (1 Corinthians 10:16). Now extend the logic of that relationship. Is not our ministry, our preaching, our witnessing, our healing, helping, counselling, the entire spectrum of our activity as Christians, a participation in Christ's continuing activity? We are continuously, moment-by-moment, being 'saved' by Christ. By his death he saves us into his present life which he adds to our lives by bringing us continuously to the Father. This is what it means to say, 'We have a witness, advocate, intercessor, friend' in Jesus Christ.

The master-picture which includes all these insights is the one of Christ as our great high priest (Hebrews 4:14–16). Israel approached God through and in the high priest. When he prayed, and offered gifts and praise, all of Israel were gathered into that one man, the many-in-the-one, illustrating the great covenant principle of total identification and solidarity of the priest with his people. Then the high priest turned and faced his people on God's behalf, as God, and they looked into his well-known face and knew that they were accepted by God.

A delightful expression of this wonderful truth is found in the work of Gerard Manley Hopkins. He spoke of Christ in the Christian and the Christian in Christ:

It is as if a man said:
'That is Christ playing at me and me playing at
   Christ,
Only it is no play but truth;

That is Christ being me and me being Christ'.[3]

Therefore a Christian . . .

> Acts in God's eye what in God's eye he is –
> Christ – for Christ plays in ten thousand places,
> Lovely in limbs, and lovely in eyes not his
> To the Father through the features of men's faces.[4]

Job's sanity is saved by his glimpse into the God who is his Judge but who is also his Saviour, even though his vision drifts out of focus too soon and Job sinks back into his old despair. There is no reason why *we* should lose sight of Christ who fulfils all Job's hopes for a witness, advocate, intercessor, friend.

LIFE AUDIT

Job 18

Bildad begins a biographical sketch with a man's death (Job 18:5): a desolate affair like an empty house with its lamps and fire extinguished (see Ecclesiastes 12:1–5). Reversing the man's history, Bildad traces it back to its root and source. He was 'one who knows not God' (Job 18:21). That was the orientation of this man's life. It twisted his experiences and booby-trapped his life's path. The picture suggests a life under a sort of curse, prone to disappointment, and its final outcome a tragic waste. But (and this is why we are looking at Bildad's poem) the 'curse' was *not* imposed by God. In fact Bildad makes no mention of divine intervention or judgement of any kind.

By his own decisions and actions the man drew down the curse upon himself. The wisdom teachers were 'convinced that by every evil deed or every good deed a momentum was released which sooner or later had an effect on the author of the deed' (von Rad).[1] The author of an act, any act, is inescapably affected by the act. There is no cheating that law of our being. We are continuously making and shaping our own future by our decisions and actions. Everything we do has significance, everything matters and connects with everything else.

> Whoever of you loves life and desires to see many
> good days,
> keep your tongue from evil and your lips from
> speaking lies.
> *Psalm 34:12–13; 1 Peter 3:10–12*

Bildad's man was *not* cursed by God but he decided the outcome of his own life by his wilful defiance of God's law. It is equally true that there is nothing good which does not also result in good: 'the tongue of the wise brings healing' (Proverbs 12:18) because good words have healing powers; it is in their nature to heal (Proverbs 12:20,25; 15:1).

What, then, ought to be the outcome of our lives, who are made in the image of God? The prophets said we should be no less proficient than the animals at navigation. The ox and ass turn instinctively towards their owner and stable (Isaiah 1:2,3). Wild birds travel immense distances with unerring precision, impelled by the desire to reach 'home' (Jeremiah 8:7). Yet our own instincts for God are strangely erratic. We do not home-in on our loving Creator and Redeemer. Sin causes navigational havoc.

Renewed . . . like a crystal

'[You] have put on the new self, which is being renewed in knowledge in the image of its Creator' (Colossians 3:10). Poet Seamus Heaney says that a real poem is formed from within like a crystal, not cut on the outside like a stone. This also describes very well the way that motives, decisions, desires and actions are formed in the renewed spiritual life. New Covenant morality flows from God's action in us whereby 'I will put my laws in their minds and I will write them on their hearts' (Hebrews 8:10–12). The effect in the believer is, as Paul describes it, 'that the righteous requirements of the law might be fully met in us, who do not live according to the sinful nature but according to the Spirit' (Romans 8:4).

Therefore wisdom so grounds the heart in God that practical daily life is continuously informed and inflamed by that relationship in the Holy Spirit. In Jesus' words, a believer's heart and treasure will be in dynamic contact with God and will thereby take on a quality of everlastingness (Matthew 6:19–21). What is that 'treasure in heaven' which can, in the end, prove that our lives have not been a futile waste of time? Simply the whole round of common-place duties which are transmuted into gold by the prayer and sincere intention – 'Lord, I do this for you' (Colossians 3:17). There is continuous, inner and secret transaction between the individual and God. No one else can know about it. No power on earth can prevent it happening. As so often, George Herbert is apt:[2]

> All may of thee partake:
> Nothing can be so mean,
> Which with this tincture (for thy sake)
> Will not grow bright and clean.

Out of this inspirational root and source the life unfolds and accumulates a true wealth, 'rich towards God' (Luke 12:21) throughout its days. It is a life continuously offered up to God in love and worship. The Father is delighted to receive it, and to keep it safe for us. Thus the life takes on depth, and its texture and colouring become more and more interesting and original.

Around the back of the high altar in Ely Cathedral, if you search, you can find designs painstakingly and skilfully carved by medieval craftsmen under some of the seats and in dark corners. Clearly they were not done to please the visitor for they are not easy to find. The vision behind the work of these craftsmen was love – 'Lord, I offer this to you'. Each man was content to leave good work out of sight and unsigned because its value was in its love to and praise of God.

'The author of the act is affected by the act,' said the wisdom-teachers. For the Christian, the inspiration for the act is an overflowing love for God. Thus we are freed from a self-conscious, wearisome preoccupation with turning every act over and over, fearful lest we get it wrong. That is a nervous, analytical, cautious way of living. Overflow is, as the word suggests, quite different. It is generous, excessive, imaginative, running in all directions, exuberant, creative. This is the nature of the Holy Spirit who, like wind, fire and living water, floods our heart with his love (Romans 15:13).

> And a life with a shapely form
> With gaiety and charm
> And capable of receiving
> With grace the grace of living
> And wild moments too
> Self when freed from you.
>
> *Patrick Kavanagh*[3]

This sounds and feels right. It suggests something like Ezekiel's vision of the river flowing out from the temple into the Dead Sea, miraculously transforming it into fresh water swarming with every kind of life; like the overflowing bounty of God's grace, pouring himself out for us by the Holy Spirit to transform the poverty of our nature (Ezekiel 47:1–12).

> Feed the gaping need of my senses, give me adlib
> To pray unselfconsciously with overflowing speech
> For this soul needs to be honoured with a new dress
>   woven
> From green and blue things and arguments that
>   cannot be proven.
>
> *Patrick Kavanagh*[4]

> Awake, north wind,
>   and come, south wind!
> Blow on my garden,
>   that its fragrance may
>   spread abroad.
>
> *Song of Songs 4:16*

STARTLING DISCLOSURES

Job 19

Navigation is impossible without fixed points to reckon by. Imagine the spooky loneliness of the long-distance runner lost in unfamiliar country at night, in the fog. This is why Job's isolation is so dangerous for him. His external certainties – his relationship with God and with the community of faith – have crumbled. Without their inspiration and discipline, Job turns in upon himself, living within his skull: he feels estranged, alienated, abandoned, forgotten, a stranger, an alien, scorned, ridiculed, turned against (Job 19:13–19).

Suddenly, heaven opens and he is given another revelation of God-with-him (vv25–27). This has happened twice before (9:33; 16:19–21) and on each occasion Job was in the depths of black despair. Here again the revelation bursts through his loneliness: 'I know that my Redeemer lives' (v25).

Where do these startling disclosures come from? Bunyan's famous incident in the Interpreter's House may provide the answer:[1]

> Then I saw in my Dream that the Interpreter took Christian by the hand, and led him into a place where was a Fire burning against a wall, and one standing by it always casting much water upon it to quench it; yet did the fire burn higher and hotter. Then said Christian, 'What means this?' ... So he had him about to the backside of the wall where he saw a man with a Vessel of Oil in his hand, of

the which he did also continually cast (but secretly)
into the fire.

John Bunyan[1]

The Holy Spirit is given to us to fulfil the promise that
'God is faithful; he will not let you be tempted beyond
what you can bear. But when you are tempted, he will
also provide a way out so that you can stand up under it'
(1 Corinthians 10:13). Job must make his difficult journey,
but God will never allow the experience to crush his child.

Time after time we also may experience the mysterious
phenomenon of 'the fire burning higher and hotter' in the
midst of the greatest discouragements: the oil of the Holy
Spirit's strong love poured onto the dwindling fire of our
faith and hope. Expect it; wonder at it; give thanks for it.
The Spirit will see to it that 'you can stand up under
it' whatever Satan throws at you.

Together the three revelations of God-with-Job suggest
how the Spirit pours his encouragements into our hearts.
He reveals strong and persuasive reasons for faith and
joy, for cheerfulness and praise, reasons which bring our
feelings into line. Our moods will take orders from the
truth about Jesus Christ, revealed to us by the Holy Spirit.

In this third episode Job sees his 'Redeemer'. This word
is a translation of the Hebrew word *Go'el*. The human
Go'el in old Israel was a kinsman. If you lost your property, perhaps even fell into slavery, your nearest able-
bodied relative was obliged to be your *Go'el* (Leviticus
25:47–49). Your *Go'el* made your difficulties his own concern and responsibility. He paid your debts, restored your
life, purchased your freedom and avenged any injustice
done to you. In the book of *Ruth*, Boaz was *Go'el* for the
young widow.

God as *Go'el* redeemed his people from Egyptian bondage (Exodus 6:6–8) and from Babylonian Exile (Isaiah
43:14; 44:22–23). In personal relations he avenges wrong.
Therefore *Proverbs* warns against exploiting the weak
because 'their Defender (*Go'el*) is strong; he will take up

their case against you' (23:10–11). On those grounds and claiming a *Go'el* relationship with God, the psalmist pleads, 'Defend my cause and redeem me; preserve my life according to your promise' (Psalm 119:154). The weak could call upon, and expect, (even demand) redeeming help from the *Go'el*. Feelings had nothing to do with it. Feelings fall into line behind facts. The *Go'el* was bound by covenant relationship to come to the help of the oppressed relative.

Job penetrates the gloom to see that there is a *Go'el* for him. His life will not crumble away into nonsense but 'I will see God'.

Jesus – our Go'el

What Job saw for a moment, the New Testament cele-brates as its central theme. And it is very much more than just a striking Hebrew metaphor. God has in Christ become our 'redeeming relative', our *Go'el*. The wonderful verses in Hebrews 2:10–18 reveal Jesus (notice in *Hebrews* the frequent use of our Lord's human name) as our brother, born into our family and therefore bound to us by the covenant ties of family life (v11). Thus he is *obliged* and *duty-bound* to take all our difficulties onto himself. Every-thing we know of him in scripture is designed to convince our troubled minds that he is *qualified* to be our *Go'el* in every respect.

As our *Go'el* kinsman-redeemer Jesus came to do for us everything needed for our emancipation and restoration. To illustrate the point, take what seems to be an odd example: repentance. Surely I can at least *repent* for myself! No. T F Torrance writes, 'Sin has been so ingrained into our minds that we are unable to repent and have to repent even of the kind of repentance we bring to God'.[2] This was why Jesus submitted to John's baptism which was for repentant sinners. He waded into the Jordan with the crowds to be 'numbered with the transgressors' (Isaiah 53:12) repenting *for us*, submitting in our place to the judgement of God on sinners – begun in Jordan, completed on Cavalry, and proclaimed in the resurrection.

Therefore, 'Let us fix our eyes on Jesus, the author and perfector of our faith' (Hebrews 12:2). Everything about Christ is vicarious and redemptive. Everything about him has saving power. Everything expresses his *Go'el* relationship with us his family. Thus *our* faith is in *his* faithfulness to us. Therefore we can say, 'In my flesh I will see God' (Job 19:26) because that is our destiny, our inheritance by grace. Jesus, our *Go'el*, is the fundamental bedrock fact of our existence as Christians. Let us look at two obvious applications to daily life.

1 He will be near to you

Knowing Jesus to be related to us as our *Go'el*, we can at last answer some teasing questions. How near is he to us at the moment? Near enough to restore our lives from bondage into 'the glorious freedom of the children of God' (Romans 8:21). Where is he at the moment? Where the *Go'el* ought to be, alongside brothers and sisters who need his strong help. But how can we be sure of his nearness and his redeeming activity, when we cannot *sense* his presence? Because it is written into the *Go'el's* job description! As a plumber works with pipes, a carpenter with wood, a baker with dough, so the *Go'el* works with and for his needy family. Confront your negative feelings with the fact of Jesus as *Go'el* and see how they are transformed. 'Fix your eyes on Jesus, the author and perfector of our faith.'

2 He will keep your life

Job realises that he has a redeemer who will vindicate him in the end (Job 19:25–27). His *Go'el* will bring his life through present confusions and uncertainties into the glorious presence of God: 'I know ... I will see ... I myself ... I, and not another ...'

The nearest our society can come to 'saving us' is

through the multi-billion pound cosmetics and fitness industry. It promises to redeem us from the onslaught of wrinkles, fat, baldness, tooth decay, dry skin, creaking joints and other terrible 'sins' against the spirit of the present age. For a life which is limited to this side of the grave, youthfulness and beauty are the two most precious assets. In his poem, 'The Leaden Echo and The Golden Echo', Gerard Manley Hopkins contemplates this inevitable loss:

> . . . no waving off these most mournful messengers,
> still messengers, sad and stealing messengers of
> grey? –
> No there's none, there's none, O no there's none,
> . . . no nothing can be done
> To keep at bay
> Age and age's evils, hoar hair . . .
> Tumbling to decay . . .

So much for Max Factor and many painful hours spent in the gym! From that forlorn hope Hopkins tells us what to do:

> Come then, your ways and airs and looks . . .
> Resign them, sign them, seal them, send them,
> motion them with breath,
> . . . deliver it, early now long before death
> Give beauty back . . .
> back to God, beauty's self and beauty's giver.
> See; not a hair is, not an eyelash, not the
> least lash lost; every hair
> Is, hair of head, numbered.

And when we have entrusted everything that we are to our *Go'el* redeemer, then what?

> O why are we so haggard at the heart, so care-coiled,
> care-killed, so fagged,

So fashed, so cogged, so cumbered,
When the thing we freely forfeit is kept with fonder
    care,
Fonder a care kept than we could have kept it, kept
Far with fonder a care (and we, we should have lost
    it).

The *Go'el* Christ comes very close to bring our lives
through to their fulfillment, and with such 'fond care'.

But not a hair on your head will perish. By standing
firm you will gain life.

Luke 21:18–19

ASK AROUND

Job 20, 21

There is nothing like travel to shake up our fixed ideas about life. So, 'question those who travel' (Job 21:29). They will agree with me, says Job, that more often than not the wicked do rather well in this life (21:7–13).

From the wider perspective of Latin America, Elsa Tamez writes this remarkable tribute to Job:[1]

> The smell of death that is about you reaches our nostrils; we smell you everywhere. Your skeletal body goads us. Shreds of your corroding flesh hang from our flesh; you have infected us, brother Job, you have infected us, our families, our people. And your look of one who thirsts for justice and your breath that is soaked in wrath have filled us with courage, tenderness and hope.

The ancient soul-friend of oppressed peoples is magnificent in his thirst and wrath against injustice in a world which he still believes is governed by the God of Justice. Affluent Christians in stable societies may feel uneasy that the Job story does not solve the scandal of undeserved suffering more neatly, thereby raising the market value of Christianity in our therapeutic cultures. But neat solutions are for Zophar, Bildad and Eliphaz and their supporters. They simply are not true to the complexities of real life.

Therefore Job cites five arguments put forward by his friends and refutes each one in turn (from Robert Gordis' commentary):[2]

1 They say, 'The lamp of the wicked is snuffed out' (18:5). Job asks ironically how often that really happens (21:17–18).

2 They say, 'God stores up a man's punishment for his sons.' But why is the wicked man himself not punished? (21:19–21).

3 They say, 'Can anyone teach knowledge to God, since he judges even the highest?' Yet the evidence raises doubts about divine wisdom. Contrast the well-being of the wicked with the misery of the righteous (21:22–26).

4 They say, 'Where now is the great man's house?' But any traveller will tell you, the great house is still standing in all its splendour (21:28–29).

5 They say, 'The evil man is reserved for the day of calamity' ('wrath, judgement', taking the NIV margin reading and the Gordis translation). Job asks why the delay? Why not punish the wicked man immediately for his evil-doing (21:29–31).

The final scandal is that even in death the evildoer is given his splendid funeral: he is held up as an example of success and taken to the grave in pomp and honour (21:32–33).

In conclusion, his friends' explanations are 'nonsense and falsehood' (v34). The word translated falsehood means 'a violation of a sacred object' and it was used, for example, to describe adultery. As Job uses it here the 'sacred object' is the truth about innocent suffering.

The flaw in his friends' interpretation of suffering and blessing is their inadequate understanding of evil and wickedness. They underrate the potency and tenacity of human wickedness, indeed its perverse attractiveness. Their ideas are therefore too neat and clear-cut and fail to connect with the dark forces that cause human beings to do terrible things to one another. Job, on the other hand, is much more in awe of the powers of human wickedness. The suffering of poverty, powerlessness, oppression and discrimination is not something fated, nor is it divine retribution for sins, but often nothing more nor less than the work of the wicked who flourish even while telling God to keep out of their affairs (vv13–15,17,18; see Amos 2:6,7; 8:1–4).

People of our time know all about the effects of human wickedness and evil. The advances of the twentieth century have been stupendous and we thank God for them, but clearly something is very wrong. This has been a murderous, suicidal, cynical and disenchanted century. It cannot be mere coincidence that it has also been an idolatrous one with man as the beginning and the end of his own schemes. Through science we can know everything, through technology we can do everything, through the market we can possess everything: that is our idolatry.

> By the mid 1760s Voltaire and his informed
> contemporaries expressed the confident belief that
> torture and other bestialities practised on subjects or
> enemies were passing forever from civilised society.
> Like the Black Death and the burning of witches
> [they] would not survive the new temper of
> European enlightenment. Secularisation was the key.
> Torture and the annihilation of human communities,
> argued the philosophers, sprang directly from
> religious dogmatism . . . with the decline in the
> strength of religious creeds there would follow, said
> Voltaire, a decline in human hatreds, in the urge to
> destroy another man . . . indifference would breed
> tolerance . . . Yet today, we find ourselves in a
> culture in which the methodical use of torture
> towards political ends is widely established. We
> come immediately after a stage of history in which
> millions of men, women and children were made
> ash . . . the wide-scale reversion to torture and mass-
> murder . . . this age of the gas-oven, of the arctic
> camps, of napalm . . . we must keep vital in ourselves
> a sense of scandal so overwhelming that it affects

every significant aspect of our position in history
and society.

George Steiner[3]

We must never forget that the creatures out of the Abyss
that sting like scorpions have human faces (Revelation
9:1–7). *Revelation* goes on to give a final picture of the
sheer resilience and tenacity of evil. After Satan is chained
and sealed up in the Abyss (Revelation 20:1–3) and God's
destruction of evil seems complete, to our astonishment
he is released again: '. . . He must be set free for a short
time'. Why? Because evil has incredible powers of endurance. Satan is released, bursting forth into a last spasm of
demonic activity that calls up every vestige of evil from
'the four corners . . . like the sand on the seashore' (v8).
He is able to tap into realms beyond our imagining or
control. He comes for the final battle with God as 'Gog
and Magog' which in *Ezekiel* are the enemy who strike
when all seems safe (Ezekiel 38:2,8,11,14–16).

Only God can reach to the depths where evil is embed-
ded in the texture of human society. We cannot exorcise
the demonic from within ourselves. This truth is connec-
ted, of course, to what is called 'original sin'. It is a mystery
but, as Pascal says, 'If the mystery is unintelligible, man is
even more unintelligible without that mystery'. Pascal also
described man as 'the glory and the scum of the universe',
capable of wonderful love and goodness and also of unbe-
lievable wickedness.

Now we can see what is involved in serious discipleship
in the world. We participate in God's 'Yes' to the world,
as the Church engages with the realities of poverty and
oppression. The situation is becoming increasingly apocalyptic as the rich and the poor grow further and further
apart, and both left- and right-wing violence escalates. It
is God's world, and he is grieved and dishonoured by the
disfiguring effects of human wickedness.

However, Job's analysis of evil demands more than our

philanthropic efforts or even economic renewal. The new order requires new people.

> What God has provided for us in Jesus Christ and what the Church proclaims and embodies in its mission and evangelism is not simply an affirmation of the best people can expect in this world by way of health, liberty, peace and freedom from want. God's reign is more than human progress on the horizontal plane ... can the Church of the crucified man from Nazareth ever become a political religion, without forgetting him and losing its identity? ... The Church-in-Mission is a sign, a pointer, symbol, example or model, a foretaste of the coming kingdom, the sacrament of its anticipations in history ... called out of the world and sent into the world, the Church is challenged to be God's experimental garden on earth, a fragment of the reign of God, having the first fruits of the Spirit [Romans 8:23] as a pledge of what is to come [2 Corinthians 1:22].
>
> *David Bosch*[4]

And what does the Lord require of you?
To act justly and to love mercy and to walk humbly
    with your God.

Micah 6:8

RESTORED FOR MINISTRY

Job 22

The facts contradict Eliphaz's theory of divine justice. He could, of course, change the theory, but that would be like murdering a favourite grandmother. Instead he turns to the old ploy of adjusting the facts to fit the theory. So now we learn that Job was, after all, a bad lot (Job 22:1–11), which would explain his suffering at God's hands. His list of crimes is very surprising in view of his flawless reputation previously endorsed by God (1:8; 2:3) and even by Eliphaz himself! (4:3–4).

We expect better of Eliphaz. His desperate manoeuvrings go to show how our theories about God may blind us to the reality of the living God himself. 'You diligently study the scriptures . . . yet you refuse to come to me to have life' (John 5:39–40). Nevertheless, as we have said before, for all his myopic dogmatism Eliphaz has things of real value to express.

On personal renewal (Job 22:21–26)

Robert Gordis translates the beautiful verse 21 as 'Put yourself in harmony with him and make peace, and thus you will attain to well being'. More usually we talk and act as if harmony and peace are initiatives only God can take with us, conditions that only he can bestow and which we more or less passively receive. Yet here we are told, 'Put yourself in harmony.' This calls to mind Jude's 'Keep yourself in God's love . . .' (Jude 21). There is a strategy we can follow from our side in order to seek the incomparable blessing of harmony and peace with God. Like blind Bartimaeus who made sure he was at the side of the road that Jesus travelled (Mark 10:46–52), we also can place ourselves in the path of divine encounter. And Eliphaz is clear about how this is best done: attend to God's word, receive it deeply by meditation, keep it and make it your own through obeying it (Job 22:22):

> Mine, O Thou Lord of life, send my roots rain.
> *Gerard Manley Hopkins*

Eliphaz, the old dogmatist, is a perceptive 'spiritual director' when he makes the blessings of harmony and peace dependent upon our decision to make God the centre and treasure of life (vv23–26). Spiritual renewal, of depth and substance, requires that we are healed from our double-mindedness. So much of our spiritual exhaustion is due to double-mindedness which shatters the fundamental principle of our being: 'Love the Lord your God will all your heart . . .' (Matthew 22:37). It is much more than mere psychological indecisiveness. James describes it as a spiritual defilement, therefore 'Come near to God . . . purify your hearts you double-minded' (James 4:8). Purity of heart is to fix the heart on God and to live with him, through him and unto him (Romans 11:36).

On the ministry of intercession (Job 22:26–30)

Job's personal renewal will open for him a remarkable ministry for others. Eliphaz assures Job that when he is restored and right with God, his life will profoundly affect the course of other people's lives. His prayer life will take on unexpected power and effectiveness (v27) for God allows himself to be influenced by the prayers of those with 'clean hands' (v30). 'What you decide on will be done' (v28). The downcast will be restored through his prayers (v29); and even God's decree of punishment against 'one who is not innocent', the evil-doer, may be set aside on account of the presence, the worth, the intercession of the saints (v30).

An audacious comment on this truth, in later Judaism, goes like this: 'Said the Holy One, Blessed be He, I rule over man, and who rules over me? The saint, for I issue a decree and he sets it aside'. But is this going too far?

Yet it is this idea which underlies Abraham's pleading with God for Sodom (Genesis 18:20–33). In the end God agrees to spare the city if there are as few as ten 'righteous' people living there. It is most important to realise that Abraham is *not* trying to rescue a few good people *out* of the great mass of bad ones. He is concerned with Sodom as a whole. He is raising the question, what decides God's judgment on Sodom – the awfulness of the majority or the innocence of the few? Israel was, of course, familiar with the idea of collective guilt, the many implicated in the guilt of the one or the few (for example, Achan's sin is described as 'Israel has sinned' in Joshua 7). The Sodom episode dares to ask whether, taking it the other way round, a community can share in the merit and worth of a godly minority. Abraham pleads on the grounds that the godly few can have a saving, preserving function on behalf of the many.

Eliphaz's prediction that Job will go on to intercede effectively for sinners eventually takes an ironic turn when God calls on Job to plead for Eliphaz and friends (Job 42:7–10).

Today, our Western culture of extreme individualism makes the idea that the people of God, the Church, can exercise a vicarious preserving function in society an elusive one to grasp. Yet look at the effect of the worship and prayer of the few, the saints, in *Revelation*, which results in the divine fire being cast on the earth (Revelation 8:1–5).

It is the Cross of Christ that is the supreme aggressor. It is the fire of God that causes the trouble. What Hitler tried to do, for example, was to stamp

89

out the fire, but the real initiative belonged to the
living God. The real aggressor is the man or the
woman who prays in the name of God. The prayers
of the saints and the fire of God move the whole
course of the world. They are the most potent, the
most disturbing, the most revolutionary, the most
terrifying powers that the world knows.

T F Torrance[1]

But notice the order in Eliphaz's words to Job: first the
personal renewal; then the potent ministry of intercession.
It gives a whole new slant to our Lord's words to his
minority people in the world: 'You are the salt of the
earth'.

HANDLES

Job 23

The sheer intensity and tenacity of Job's engagement with
God (Job 23:3–10) makes him seem to the modern reader
like someone from another planet, a planet with strong
spiritual visions of life. He searches for the God ('if only
I knew where to find him', v3) who has already found him
('he knows the way I take', v10). Are we capable any
longer of that sort of sustained spiritual pursuit?

> The anxiety and violence of this present age are not
> a sign of vigour and vitality but rather of frustration
> and enfeeblement. Our desires are not too intense
> but too weak, too dissipated and undirected.
>
> E L Mascall[1]

It is hardly in keeping with the spirit of the times to take
God so seriously. In Robertson Davies' novel, *The Cornish
Trilogy*,[2] the artist Saraceni argues with a friend:

> Very well. Live in the spirit of your times and that
> spirit alone if you must. But for some artists
> abandonment to the contemporary leads to despair.
> Men, today, men without religion or mythology solicit
> the Unconscious and usually they ask in vain. So
> they invent something and I don't need to tell you
> the difference between invention and inspiration.

There is a danger that we duck the awkward mysteries of
our faith by too easily lumping them together in a box

labelled 'Jesus is the Answer'. Indeed, he is, but it was the Holy Spirit of Christ who went to great lengths to bring us this strange drama we call the book of *Job*. The response 'Jesus is the Answer' may be due more to laziness or even fear than to confident faith.

Job has come upon further interpretations of his difficulties, which are like handles. How difficult and dangerous it is to try and left a boiling saucepan off the stove if the thing does not have an handle! Similarly, we need a way of bringing our experiences closer for inspection and interpretation. We need handles and here are some of Job's.

Slow gold – but everlasting

'When he has tested me, I shall come forth as gold' (v10). Job can see God as a refiner of precious metals who melts the gold in order to burn off the dross and thereby raise its value. The picture refers, says H H Rowley[3], more exactly to the shining surface of the molten gold in the crucible after the impurities are removed. Great heat is required for that process. For the believer, the fire is the heat and trials of experience.

The fires of God (for that is what our experiences become in his hands) are never merely capricious flames. They represent the saving and sanctifying activity of God whose uncompromising and purposeful love intends beautiful qualities and designs in his people.

> Nothing is inexorable but love. Love which will yield to prayer is imperfect and poor. Nor is it then the love that yields, but its alloy . . . For love loves unto purity. Love has ever in view the absolute loveliness of that which it beholds. Where loveliness is incomplete; and love cannot love its fill of loving, it spends itself to make more lovely, that it may love more; it strives for perfection, even that itself may be perfected – not in itself, but in the object . . .

Therefore all that is not beautiful in the beloved,
all that comes between and is not of love's kind,
must be destroyed. And our God is a consuming
fire.

George Macdonald[4]

The fire is necessary to refine and purify the gold. Yet in
one important respect God acts differently from the
ancient goldsmith who separated the gold from the dross.
Because of the severe heat of the furnace the goldsmith
would stand well back, operating the bellows from outside
the furnace walls. Yet Israel, in the fire of her Babylonian
captivity, for example, discovered that God was with her
in it (Daniel 3). The terrible fire of Nebuchadnezzar's
furnace was at the same time the fire of God, made so by
the fourth figure who 'looks like a son of the gods' (Daniel
3:25).

Job's experiences have much in common with Israel's
exile – bewilderment, anguish, a sense of being betrayed
by God, pain and humiliation. Both Job and Israel felt
compelled to seek daring new interpretations of divine
providence. Job's realisation of value and purpose, emerging out of apparently destructive experiences, aligns with
God's word to Israel: 'Fear not . . . I will be with you . . .
When you walk through the fire, you will not be burned;
the flames will not set you ablaze' (Isaiah 43:1,2).

The fire is, in fact, the consuming love of God at work
in the people who reflect him to the world. The three
young men in the Babylonian furnace were representative
Israelites. In *Malachi* the representative priests were pur-
ified because they were priests (Malachi 3:3–4). Job was
in his own way a representative man. Robert Gordis translates verse 14: 'He will surely carry out what he had
decreed for me – and He has many more such cases!'
meaning that Job is Everyman and his experiences
encompass those of all people. The Church of Jesus Christ
is now his representative people mirroring the divine
nature to the world, no less loved by God than the Old

Testament saints and therefore no less in the refiner's crucible.

> He is a consuming fire, that only that which cannot be consumed may stand forth eternal. It is the nature of God, so terribly pure that it destroys all that is not pure as fire, which demands like purity in our worship. He will have purity. It is not that the fire will burn us if we do not worship thus; but that the fire will burn us until we worship thus; yea, will go on burning within us after all that is foreign to it has yielded to its force, no longer with pain and consuming, but as the highest consciousness of life, the presence of God.
>
> *George Macdonald*

It is, of course, a slow process. Nothing whizz-bang about the purifying of precious metals! In Emily Dickinson's lovely phrase we are 'slow gold – but everlasting', which is yet another handle to enable us get a hold on the mystery of events, bring them closer for reflection and admire the divine goldsmith at his business.

THE 'POOR MAN' TAKES CENTRE-STAGE

Job 24

Job's picture of the weak and the poor suffering at the hands of the powerful could draw blood from a stone (Job 24:2–12). Here is the 'thirst for justice and your breath soaked in wrath' that so impressed Elsa Tamez in Peru (page 82). Yet it is not easy to stay outraged. Take the case of the teenager recently who found she was quite unmoved by pictures of the Holocaust: not a heartless or wicked person, but morally desensitised by too much TV/video 'entertainment' violence. Familiarity breeds consent. We are awash with terrible images similar to the suffering Job describes, beamed into our homes from around the world. As for those 'friends of darkness' (vv13–17), they sound pretty ordinary to us – we who are drowning in our own crime-wave!

Yet we must respond. We must, if only for the sake of our own humanity. The psychologist William James wrote, 'If you are moved by a sonnet or a sunset you must do something about it, even if it is only to kiss your grandmother'. Inactivity in the face of urgent information paralyses the soul. If I am touched but fail to respond, soon I will not be able to respond. Jesus said, 'Now that you *know* these things, you will be blessed if you *do* them' (John 13:17).

As Christians we must respond and so witness to the justice, mercy and love of God. Job is wrong to implicate God in the scandal of man's inhumanity to man (Job 24:1,

12). The prophets denounced the mistreatment of the poor and the weak as an outrage of economics and ethics. In the Bible, the 'poor man' takes centre-stage in God's concerns for the world. Consider Isaiah 65:20–23, the Isaiah Agenda, as an answer to Job's oppressed people:[1]

> Never again will there be in it
>> an infant who lives but a few days
>>> or an old man who does not live out his years;
> he who dies at a hundred
>> will be thought a mere youth;
> he who fails to reach a hundred
>> will be considered accursed.
> They will build houses and dwell in them;
> they will plant vineyards and eat their fruit.
> No longer will they build houses and others live in
>> them, or plant and others eat.
> For as the days of a tree,
>> so will be the days of my people;
> my chosen ones will long enjoy
>> the works of their hands.
> They will not toil in vain
>> or bear children doomed to misfortune;
> for they will be a people blessed by the Lord,
>> they and their descendants with them.

Is Isaiah describing paradise only? He certainly expressed the truth about God's hopes for his world. So, if we ask, 'What is God doing in the world? What does he want to see? What gives him great pleasure?', we can draw our answers from Isaiah's vision. To work towards that vision reveals the heart of God, helps to make him known in the world, and is to do his will.

Our efforts to practice Isaiah's vision, to incarnate God's justice and love, our programmes for relief, education, healing, feeding the hungry and creating a proper self-sufficiency in life, are all a witness. They point, like a signpost, beyond themselves to the living God who is revealed in those acts of love and justice: the bread speaks of the one who is the Bread. Without this character of witness our efforts are futile (John 6:32–35). God's passion for justice and mercy for the poor should be incarnated in his people. Are they?

THE POWER OF AN ADORING MIND

Job 25 – 27

These 'wisdom' people are fascinating. Several times we have criticised the way they keep to the tramlines of their dogmatism. They sift through life's experiences to come up with a blueprint for the Good Life. It's all a bit too neat and tidy for our liking.

Yet these people glide from their dogmatism into high adoration from one moment to the next. Their problem-solving minds ignite into worshipping minds. They do their careful thinking on the edge of praise. The dogmatists are hymnists. Thus Bildad responds to Job's latest outburst with a hymn celebrating the 'dominion and awe' of God (Job 25:1–6 and continued in 26:7–14). Time and again the thought and speech of these men passes into adoration. What is the secret of their spirituality?

Exploring the mystery

They try to penetrate creation as the sphere of God's ways (26:7–13). We glorify God when we investigate his handiwork, but very soon we are up against mystery. However intently we peer into a well, we learn nothing of its depth. All we see is our own reflection in its surface. The world we want to crack open eludes our grasp and vanishes into the mist of vast divine mysteries that surround our existence in every aspect.

Later Elihu makes great play of the mysterious wonder of the God who eludes our grasp and who is beyond our control (36:26–29; 37:5,14–19,23): 'Tell us what we should say to him; we cannot draw up our case because of our darkness'. Yet 'our darkness' is not felt to be benightedness, a frustration, or in any sense a depressing failure. 'It is the glory of God to conceal a matter,' says the wisdom teacher (Proverbs 25:2), therefore we will approach God in a humble, adoring spirit.

In the developed world, our instinct (for we are the children of a technically brilliant, 'can-do' culture) is to try and draw events and phenomena towards us into the light of our rational clarity where we can investigate them. Sooner or later, however, we reach a point when things seem to reverse and slip away from us into mystery. For example, a man falls in love and seems to have hit upon the secret of happiness and the reason for living. Then his lover dies and the very thing that seemed to illuminate his entire existence goes into reverse and disappears into impenetrable darkness. We very quickly reach the limits and boundaries in our unaided search for a way of living with mystery.

Faced with this baffling enigma, the wisdom teachers advise us to seek the Lord with an adoring mind, to make a big thing of our ignorance.

> I am the most ignorant of men;
>> I do not have a man's understanding.
> I have not learned wisdom,
>> nor have I knowledge of the Holy One.
> Who has gone up to heaven and come down?
>> Who has gathered up the wind in the hollow of
>> his hands?
> Who has wrapped up the waters in his cloak?
>> Who has established all the ends of the earth?
> What is his name, and the name of his son?
>> Tell me if you know!
>
> Every word of God is flawless;
>> he is a shield to those who take refuge in him.
>>>>> *Proverbs 30:2–5*

In New Testament terms, the writer is acknowledging that he is 'poor in spirit' because he cannot grasp the mystery of life. And he 'mourns' because he has no mastery of life. He stands naked without any pretence before the One 'in whom are hidden all the treasures of wisdom and knowledge' (Colossians 2:3). God promises that such a seeker will not go away empty-handed (Matthew 5:3–4).

We will approach God with an adoring mind because only such a mind is attuned to think about God.

'God cannot be known except by devotion'

> The perfect knowledge of God is so to know him that we are sure that we must not be ignorant of him, yet cannot describe him. We must believe, we must apprehend, must worship; and such acts of devotion must stand in place of definition.
>
> *Bishop Hilary*[1]

In other words, the nature of the One we think about must be allowed to determine the way we think about him. This is nicely illustrated in the quaint old idea that the eye can see the sun because the eye is the same shape as the sun! The holy, adorable God will reveal himself to the holy, adoring worshipper.

Bildad reveals something of this attitude. How little we tiny mortals understand (Job 25:6). We investigate atoms and molecules, genes and galaxies but what we see in the beautiful things of creation is only 'the outer fringe of his works; how faint the whisper we hear of him! Who then can understand the thunder of his power?' (26:14). Behind the visible 'fringe' of things, the Creator exercises his authority by subduing the 'powers and authorities' which threaten chaos and disruption, pictured in the mythological Rahab and the dragon (26:12,13; Isaiah 51:9). John used the same imagery for Christ in his incarnation, mortally wounding the Satan-Dragon, the great Disrupter of

Creation (Revelation 12). Thus the source of our life and joy and light is found beyond the 'outer fringes of his works'. We know it is there, out of sight, beyond our natural reach, because in scripture God 'whispers' of this great reality. Only the humble, believing, worshipping mind can enter into its understanding and live with the thunder of his power. Only the God-attuned mind can receive the mind of God (1 Corinthians 2:9–16). Hence the famous principle that the saints have sent down to us: believe in order to understand (see John 8:31–32).

Like a dove in a valley

However far we progress into the mystery of God, his love and truth and beauty, each point we reach is a starting point for our journey to the next.

Gregory of Nyssa compared the believer to a dove flying along a valley. The end of the valley, as it appears from a distance, seems to be a dead end, blocked by a mountain. However, when the dove reaches the mountain wall, it discovers that there is a way around it into another valley which also appears to be a cul-de-sac, until, again, the dove arrives at the end and finds another valley, and so on. Each time what was apparently the end becomes the starting point for the next exploration.

The frame of heart and mind, which allows us to move on and on like this, is a sense of awe at the mystery and wonder of God. A praising mind will open up valleys to us.

WHERE IS WISDOM?

Job 28

The situation cries out for a fresh touch. The debate between Job and his friends is stuck in a weary deadlock. They have had their final say, and Job has replied with undiminished sarcasm (Job 26:1–4). And still there is God. Where can Job go in his argument with the God who will not even answer him?

Revelation arrives in the majestic hymn to wisdom and the timing is perfect. Here is a hopeful way of assessing the various opinions and arguments about suffering. Are they 'wise'? And, more exactly, how can we get in touch with 'wisdom'?

Wisdom is . . .

We start with the fact that the whole world is the creation of God:

> How many are your works, O Lord!
> In wisdom you made them all . . .
> > *Psalm 104:24*

> By wisdom the Lord laid the earth's foundations . . .
> > *Proverbs 3:19*

Not merely that the wise Creator has created wisely, but that the world possesses wisdom as an attribute. Wise orderliness is in the nature of creation, poured into it, bestowed upon it, imprinted in its texture.

We experience the impact of wisdom upon us when we

look into creation and feel the rhyme and reason of things, order, meaning, the way things are. The wisdom teachers, particularly in *Job*, realised that creation was one of God's languages and that, along with prophets and priests, it was a voice which could reach men and women. Hans Wolff writes, 'The truth that knowledge of the world can be wisdom for men and women is founded objectively on the world as creation'.[1] So handle it with care; attend to what God is saying to you through it.

Wisdom is not the same as information and knowledge.

> All our knowledge brings us nearer to our ignorance,
> All our ignorance brings us nearer to death,
> But nearness to death no nearer to GOD.
> Where is the Life we have lost in living?
> Where is the wisdom we have lost in knowledge?
> Where is the knowledge we have lost in information?
> *T S Eliot*[2]

These are timely questions as society cruises along the super-highway of information technology! Three pictures in *Proverbs* describe wisdom:

1 Wisdom – the woman in the city

She is a woman walking the city: 'Wisdom calls aloud in the street, she raises her voice in the public squares; at the head of the noisy streets she cries out . . .' Wisdom is calling to anyone with enough sense to attend (Proverbs 1:20–27). She throws a party and, like the Gospel invitation, whosoever will may come (Proverbs 9:1–6). Wisdom's call is not to the special or philosophically-minded few. No snobbery or elitism with her. She stands at the most prominent positions, on high points and at crossroads, at the city gates (Proverbs 8:1–21). She promises life, God's favour (8:35) and security (1:33). What in practical terms can all this mean?

We find that there is a created correspondence between the world 'out there' and the way we perceive it 'in here'. Wisdom-in-creation addresses our innate desires for order, progress, design, health, fulfilment, 'success'. Or conversely, she responds to our dread of chaos, meaningless, destruction and a life that threatens to crumble away into nonsense.

Wisdom-in-creation calls to our inner, personal life (Proverbs 2:9–20) promising to lead us into 'every good path' because she can impart the discernment by which to choose 'wisely'. Wisdom operates in the wider world also. She is the directing influence in society, superior to power and wealth (Proverbs 24:1–6). Hence wisdom's attack upon militarism and all acts of violence (Proverbs 16:32). She does not offer an escapist flight from the real world but, instead, offers a better way of conducting public and political affairs.

'A wise man attacks the city of the mighty and pulls down the stronghold in which they trust' (Proverbs 21:22). Similarly, with economic affairs (Proverbs 16:16). Wisdom's laws and principles permeate our everyday life and we misunderstand them at our peril.

2 Wisdom – the master craftsman

Wisdom is God's master craftsman, who was with him 'before the world began'(Proverbs 8:22–31). This picture emphasises the idea of the design and structure of physical life. Good architecture and sound construction is one example (Proverbs 24:3–4), also the skill in fashioning metals (1 Kings 7:14, AV – 'he was filled with wisdom, and understanding, and cunning to work all works in brass') goldsmith's work and wood carving (Exodus 31:3, AV) and in spinning (Exodus 35:25, AV). Thus the skilled worker is often called 'wise' because in his work he is tapping into the truth which is 'there' in nature. In that sense an accomplished seaman is also called 'wise' (Ezekiel 27:8, translated 'skilled' in the NIV).

We delight in perceiving the Master Craftsman's shaping touch in the incredible beauty, awesome power and breathtaking ingenuity of design in the natural order. Conversely, witness our sense of profound loss, distress, even bereavement if through human stupidity or greed, the Craftsman's organising voice is ignored and nature is turned into a rubbish tip.

3 Wisdom – the favourite child

In another translation of the same passage (Proverbs 8:22–31) wisdom is described as being with God in pre-creation life, a vivacious youngster full of laughter, who delights in God's presence and loves to play with the human family in the playground of the world. Wisdom as the playful child speaks of beauty, the mysterious gift of language and communication, art, drama, literature, music, poetry – the life of the imagination and creativity, and all that comes within the aesthetic delight of life.

But there is nothing cut and dried about these representations. Wisdom is a reality which is hidden in profound mystery. Wisdom permeates all created things. It is part of the way in which God rules providentially in the world, and nobody, least of all the atheist, can escape its presence, its call and effect upon them. What Isaiah's seraphim claimed for the glory of God – that it 'fills' the whole earth – applies equally to wisdom (Isaiah 6). Therefore the Psalmist can say that the heavens declare, the skies proclaim, the day speaks, the night displays, their voice goes out (Psalm 19). Job himself has already appealed to wisdom-in-creation: 'ask the animals ... speak to the earth, and it will teach you' (Job 12:7–10).

If these thoughts strike you as altogether too 'Green' or even 'New Age', it shows how far we have neglected this mighty wisdom teaching in scripture, thereby surrendering the high ground of creation theology to sub-Christian ideologies.

'Get wisdom'

Obviously, whatever else we think is essential for real life, we must heed the urgent call to 'get wisdom' (Proverbs 4:5).

> If a man wants to manifest himself as God's image and therefore as a good steward of creation and a good administrator of history, he has to reject the crimes of stupidity and foolishness; he needs enlightenment through the wisdom which permeates all the decisions of life.
>
> *Hans Wolff*[3]

In fact this comment should flash an urgent warning to us. Our situation is not that we simply need a few pointers to get ourselves phased-in with wisdom. We are sinners and our capacity to discern and go with wisdom is seriously damaged. We continually misread life. We mistake the mirage for the pool, time after time. Thus, on the one hand, our own humanity in all its wonderful abilities is evidence of the imprint of wisdom:

> . . . what may be known about God is plain . . . For since the creation of the world God's invisible qualities – his eternal power and divine nature – have been clearly seen, being understood from what has been made . . .
>
> *Romans 1:18–20*

On the other hand, in the next verses Paul writes:

> . . . their thinking became futile and their foolish hearts were darkened. Although they claimed to be wise, they became fools . . .
>
> *Romans 1:21–32*

Hence, realistically, wisdom for us is now personified

in Jesus Christ, our 'saving wisdom'.

'Christ . . . wisdom from God'

Christ fulfills the lovely images in *Proverbs* – the woman, the craftsman, the playful child. They are the background to the New Testament teaching that he is the Word of God through whom everything is created, held in harmony and brought to God's intended fulfilment (John 1:1–4; Colossians 1:15–20; Hebrews 1:1–3). And the Wisdom-Word is – by his incarnation, death on the cross, and his resurrection – our 'saving wisdom' by whose power we are restored, healed, renewed in our capacity to live wisely. (See 1 Corinthians 1:18 – 2:16 for our restoration to wisdom by the cross and the Holy Spirit.)

'But where can wisdom be found?'

Only now are we ready for the thrust of this great wisdom poem (Job 28:1ff). The mining enterprise is a potent symbol of man's powers to seek out and possess whatever he sets his heart on. The great heroic qualities are there: courage, ingenuity, endurance, intelligence, comradeship and sheer drive. These enable the miner to bring to the surface the most inaccessible minerals. He 'brings hidden things to light' (v11). But wisdom, the most precious commodity of them all, cannot be found in this way (vv12,20). It sounds like a cruel joke. We cannot grasp the thing we cannot live without.

But it is no cruel trick, or game of cosmic hide-and-seek. The key to wisdom belongs with God. He is its keeper. Wisdom, as we have already seen, is not a body of knowledge we could possess independently of God. God 'understands the way to it' (v23) because he *is* it. 'The fear of the Lord, that is wisdom' (v28).

Yet wisdom and fear (awe, reverence) are not identical. *Proverbs* says, 'The fear of the Lord *teaches* a man wisdom' (Proverbs 15:33). This is the key 'for the Lord gives wisdom, and from his mouth come knowledge and understanding' (Proverbs 2:6). Only from 'his mouth', from scripture, can we know that the world is his creation. Only because God speaks these marvellous things in scripture do we have the faith and courage to entrust ourselves to the principles which we discern in that word. Only God can give us the openness to his world that we need to encounter his wisdom there; only he can save us from 'inwardly distorted foolishness' (Wolff). Our ability to perceive wisdom is as much God's gift as wisdom-in-creation itself (James 1:5–8).

Thus the 'fear of the Lord' brings us back again to love, respect and adoration towards him as a habit of mind. If this is our inner orientation – utter dependence upon God – then we are promised participation in his wisdom. Anyone who thinks they can, by their own powers, penetrate the veil of mystery that covers the total reality of the world, is lost in an illusion of their own making (Job 26:12–14).

Therefore, humility is wisdom's twin (Proverbs 8:12,13) just as pride is the twin of foolishness: 'For arrogance which abandons the fear of God also robs man of his future. Only the humble remains truly man, for wisdom sets him on the true path of the fear of the Lord' (Wolff). Such wise humility involves habitual, attentive listening to the call of God's word, a desire to concur with every new thing we discover about him. Humility gives a directing spiritual energy and a distinctive slant to the mind, inspiring and shaping thought and imagination. Wisdom is the spin-off, the incidental by-product of our love and adoration for God. It is the spiritual (and Spirit-given) ability to see to the heart of things, to know what makes life tick. If we are wise, we will neither despise creation nor worship it, but relate to it in truth and with spiritual intelligence.

> We shall behold the centres,
>> know their uses,
>>> see every property,

every excellence,
Every degree in every excellence,
Every end to which they are ordained,
Every person to whom they relate . . .
Thomas Traherne[4]

GOD'S SPECIAL CONCERN

Job 29 – 31

We turned aside briefly to look to Isaiah's Agenda for a response to the heart-rending sufferings of the powerless described by Job in chapter 24. Now we encounter this lovely description of compassion for the poor. Nostalgia may have inflated Job's memory somewhat, but his concern for the weak has the ring of truth to it. Let us take it at face value and ponder some of the striking things he says.

To dress in 'righteousness' and 'justice' (Job 29:14) is neither an abstract idea nor a matter of individual piety. Above all else, it is the practical defence of the defenceless. 'Orphans, widows and strangers' (vv 12,13,16) is the biblical term for the poor and the powerless, and Job is concerned for other innocent sufferers (30:25). The powerless are God's special concern. We may puzzle why he allows exploitation of the weak but there is no doubt at all what he wants us to do about it. 'Father to the needy' (Job 29:16) is one of God's own titles (Psalm 68:5) which Job has taken as the standard for his own concern. Gordis translates the rest of verse 16: 'a helpless one, whom I did not know, I searched out', which connects in our minds with the dangerous, time-consuming and practical love of the good Samaritan for the innocent victim (Luke 10:25–37).

Here is the logic of our faith: God's boundless generosity to us in Christ makes boundlessly generous people out of us. Thus we also put on 'righteousness' and 'justice'. He is that kind of God, and his people should be like him (1

John 4:9–11). Righteousness and justice challenge us to defend or restore rights that have been violated, especially on behalf of the powerless who are in no position to defend themselves. It is one of the great biblical commandments because it arises from the heart of God (see Micah 6:8).

Everything altered by Exodus

'Father to the needy.' Only Isaiah gives the term such a wide meaning (Isaiah 22:21). Especially in legal cases the poor needed protection from the 'fangs of the wicked' (Job 29:17), the voracious people who seized onto them. It was here that Job gave his help (vv7–12), not only with material assistance (easy for a wealthy man to do without much thought) but also in the far more demanding and time-consuming task of obtaining justice and mercy for the powerless in the courts.

This is godliness because God is like this (eg James 1:27). Our values, ethics, politics and behaviour should reflect the way God has dealt with us in Christ. The status of master and slave was grounded in Israel's fundamental experience of God in the Exodus (Deuteronomy 5:14,15; 15:12–18). The principle was always 'remember that you were slaves in Egypt and the Lord your God redeemed you', therefore deal generously with other people. He frees you; work to free others (Job 29:12).

Every relationship we have is radically affected by Christ's Exodus love which reveals the value that God places upon every person (Job 31:13–15; Malachi 2:10).

What does it say for the unique quality of our human nature when God Almighty can clothe himself with it, yet remain God? What price is placed on every human being by the fact that Christ gave his life to ransom them from their sins? Can we ever explain the mysterious depths and potential of our human nature when God the Holy Spirit chooses to make the human body his temple and from there to renew it 'in knowledge in the image of its Creator' (Colossians 3:10)? We cannot take our estimation of a human being from fashionable political correctness, or sentimental notions, or the images which come to us via the media. Our worth was established two thousand years ago when God so loved the world that he gave . . .

Even a sort of ecological justice in relation to the earth is recognised here (Job 31:38–40).

Finally, Job recognises a profound and fundamental connection between God, neighbour and money, which can be corrupted into idolatry, greed and abuse of neighbour (31:16–28). If we idolatrously exchange 'the glory of the immortal God for images' (Romans 1:23), our attitudes to money and people are destabilised as a consequence. Then we overvalue things and tend to regard other people in a derogatory, remote, exploitative way.

How can we recognise that we have fallen into this kind of idolatry, given that we have not actually set up a totem pole in our backyard? In terms of these chapters in *Job* (chapters 24, 29–31) we might reconstruct the truth about God to make him into a deity who somehow floats above this messy world, only concerned to save that part of us we call our souls, a very 'spiritual' God in fact. Clearly this is a lie, a blasphemous misrepresentation of God.

> A father to the fatherless, a defender of widows,
>   is God in his holy dwelling.
> God sets the lonely in families,
>   he leads forth the prisoner with singing . . .
>   *Psalm 68:5,6*

WINESKINS AND DREAMS

Job 32 – 37

Job and his friends have run out of arguments. We can wait no longer to hear from God who has yet to answer and resolve the discussion. The young newcomer, Elihu, follows much the same tack as Zophar, Bildad and Eliphaz (and at great length!) except in one respect. For anyone interested in the way God moves in people to communicate through them, Elihu has several powerful and original things to say.

'Full of words . . . ready to burst' (Job 32:15–22)

In a culture where age was synonymous with wisdom the young knew their place and kept quiet. Listen and learn (32:6–7). On this model, wisdom comes by long years of experience and reflection, like a battery steadily charged which is able to give out a steady light.

However, Elihu feels such divine pressure on his spirit that he has no choice but to break that etiquette. He is like a wineskin in danger of bursting if the violent fermentation of the wine within it is not ventilated. Elihu is 'full of words and the spirit within [him] compels [him]' (v18). Eliphaz had described his prophetic vision in careful, serene terms (4:12), but this young man is so full of uncontrollable energy and drive that he simply 'must speak and find relief' (v20). Here, it is the effect of the message on the speaker that is important, not how it strikes the listener (v21). Elihu is indignant and angry at the way, as he saw it, Job dishonoured God with his criticisms

(32:3–5). John Ruskin once complained that people no longer seem capable of this sort of anger: 'we have starved and chilled our faculty of indignation'. Perhaps our problem today is that we have grown too tolerant, too balanced and quick to see all sides of every question. Or is it in fact something more sinister, a loss of nerve and conviction which simply masquerades as broadmindedness?

'God does speak – now one way, now another' (Job 33:14–19)

Elihu rejects Job's complaint that God has remained silent throughout (32:12,13). Is God ever really silent, or is it that we control the ways in which he can communicate with us (v14)? We each have our traditions of hearing, a range of attention, a spectrum of divine communication which is too limiting. God holds the initiative in how and when he speaks with us. He is Lord of all creation, and all creation reveals his word. We saw it in the way wisdom (the playful child, master craftsman, the woman in the city) is imprinted on the texture of creation, calling out to men and women with enough sense to come in out of the rain.

God's thunder and his whisper, his clout and his caress, his self-disclosure and his hiddenness, through the passionate sermon and through the chance remark overheard in the supermarket, can speak to us 'now one way, now another' (1 Kings 19:7–12). He can speak to us even through states of mind in which we are powerless to effect things, psychically extraordinary forms such as dreams (Job 33:15,16) 'when the outward eye is closed in the night of unconsciousness and in its place the inner eye opens up to behold the mysteries of the divine realm' (Eichrodt). Dream-messages are prone to abuse. Jeremiah condemned the prophets' fascination with them (Jeremiah 23:25–29), comparing word and dream to grain and straw. Yet dreams can be a medium of authentic divine communication. I should like to mention two personal instances.

In a home-meeting recently, I asked a woman how she had come to personal faith. It began, she said, with a dream when she was twelve. In it she saw a man ('as clearly as I see you sitting here') standing in front of five arches. Some forty years later, one day she heard a knock at the door, opened it and saw the man standing there. She recognised him at once as the man standing in front of the five arches in her dream. It was the new minister. She and her husband later came to personal faith in Christ under his ministry. But what of the five arches? Only recently she was working in the church on the carpet in front of the altar. She lifted up the altar covers and there saw five arches carved into the old stone altar. Each Sunday the minister stands in front of five arches.

My Thai language teacher in Thailand, a thoughtful Bhuddist, became a Christian through a dream. We regularly studied the Gospels together, and the truth about Jesus was played out powerfully for him in a dream one night in which Jesus saved him from a terrifying demon. It convinced him.

God can also speak through distress (Job 33:19,22) when, as in dreams, we are utterly unable to control our circumstances.

We should never say, 'God couldn't possibly speak in this or that way' or 'He can only speak in such and such a way.' Our part is to be open, with our inner life tuned to the Holy Spirit, so that we are sensitive to his touch and his word when and however it comes. '*Not revelation it is that waits, but our unfurnished eyes*' (Emily Dickinson).

THE ANSWER

Job 38 – 42:6

At last God answers Job. The angry rebel is ready, expecting, demanding an explanation which would make sense of his weird experiences. He has raged against God, but only because he believes in God. Not once throughout the entire drama has Job yielded to unbelief. Doubt, yes, often, but never unbelief. This is an important distinction for our own spiritual journey.

> Doubts are the messengers of the Living One to the honest. They are the first knock at our door of things that are not yet, but have to be, understood . . . Doubt must precede every deeper assurance; for uncertainties are what we first see when we look into a region hitherto unknown, unexplored, unannexed.
>
> *George Macdonald*[1]

Now God speaks. Standing in Job's shoes we might reasonably expect two things about the reply. First, that the Lord would take pencil and paper to show how that and that difficult experience had this and this significance. And second, that God might be just a little bit apologetic for all the anguish he had put us through. But not a bit of it!

The diagnosis

Before moving to his astonishing answer, God first takes Job's argument apart and points out two serious flaws which have developed.

First, Job's words, their quantity and effect, so many and so furious, spraying ignorance around all over the place like a rusty Sten gun: 'Who is this that darkens my counsel with words without knowledge?' (Job 38:2). Here 'counsel' refers to the divine plan and purpose in creation (Job 12:13; Proverbs 8:14), the way God manages his world (Isaiah 5:19; 46:10).

Second, the effect of Job's criticism would be to restrict God's freedom to enact his purposes in the world: 'Would you discredit my justice? Would you condemn me to justify yourself?' (Job 40:8).

The two charges amount to the same thing, that Job is interfering in the way God runs his affairs. The shop assistant has been out of touch with the proprietor for so long that he starts treating the shop as his own. It is as if God is a guest in our world rather than the other way around.

You think it could not happen to us? Just listen in any prayer meeting. We invite God into our schemes and events as if they did not exist until we invented them. Yet the higher truth is that our thinking and imagining, when they *are* creative and on target, merely realise and *participate in* the thoughts and imaginings of God. A lovely definition of the Church is a community in which are planted seeds of God's imagination.

We do not 'activate' God each morning by our prayers. He has been busy throughout the night working out 'everything in conformity with the purpose of his will' (Ephesians 1:11). We can sleep because he never does. Our wisest prayer is for grace to discern and participate in God's counsel in the world: 'For we are God's workmanship, created in Christ Jesus to do good works, which God prepared in advance for us to do' (Ephesians 2:10).

A sign that we may have disastrously shifted from serving God in the vineyard to seizing control of it (Luke 20:9–18) is in the sense of strain which is so prevalent in our Evangelical life. Playing God is an exacting role which we were never designed to undertake. As a Japanese Emperor said, 'I've had so many worries since becoming god.' We pay a high price for interfering 'without knowledge' in God's affairs.

Now to the answer. Job is invited to take a seat for the greatest multi-media show of them all, and to listen carefully to the commentary.

The carnival

God parades creation past Job for his admiration. Observe its design, structure, function: the world and the stars; the mysterious power and wisdom permeating the whole performance and carrying everything forward to its goal; the animals in all their variety – beautiful or odd, terrifying or comic.

Throughout the procession we hear the voice of the commentator, the Creator himself. There is no reference at all to Job's long and anguished questions. Instead God fires off a stream of unanswerable counter-questions. Were you there? What do you know? Can you tell? Have you ever? Teach me, you who are so clever. Can you do it? You who have lived so long and seen so much. Supremely ironic, the counter-questions clearly show that God has rejected Job's complaints against him (von Rad).[2]

It is a strange answer which seems not to answer anything directly. What are we to make of it?

First, that clearly it has an enormous effect on Job himself. Something clicks and leaves him utterly awestruck (Job 42:1–6). The old anger, hurt, resentment and all his righteous indignation are not answered but dissolve within the profound disclosure that God makes in his response.

In his speech God entrusts creation with the task of leading Job back to the mystery behind creation. Is creation up to the task?

> God allows creation, that is, someone other than himself, to speak for him. He lets these other things speak and causes them to speak . . . eloquently of themselves. He obviously counts upon it that they belong so totally to him, that they are so subject to him and at his disposal, that in speaking of themselves they will necessarily speak of him . . . He is so sure of them as his creatures . . . to be sure at once of the service which the creatures will quite simply render him in his self-manifestation.
>
> *Karl Barth*[3]

This says the most wonderful things about the created order as parable, sign, riddle, and leads the determined, humble seeker to the Creator standing within it all.

Very well, let the carnival begin. We will observe the things and animals, listen to those 'machine-gun' questions that punctuate their appearance and, hopefully, we will discern clues to God's ways with men and women.

They speak of order and purpose, of cosmos not chaos, of foundations laid carefully before superstructures (Job 38:4–6) of boundaries and limits and discipline (vv8–11) so as to release the earth for fruitfulness and harvest.

Is it chance
Or dance moves
    the world?

Is the world
Blind and dumb
    or bloom, festal?

> A vain jest,
>   or holy feast?
>
> *Eugene Warren*[4]

The great German astronomer, Johan Kepler (1571–1630), spoke of seventeenth century scientists as approaching their work worshipfully 'as priests officiating around the altar of the Creator' and their science as a vehicle to the 'seraphic love' of God. Ponder the significance (the 'sign') of the regularity and consistency of the daily pattern, the dawn when 'the earth takes shape like clay under a seal' (Job 38:12–14). Order, purpose, beauty and patterns create freedom for life to teem in the dance of creation. They point to the nature of a God who has made a covenant with his creation (eg Genesis 8:22). The fact that Jesus, the Son of God, took our flesh upon himself and, by the power of the resurrection, brought it from the grave into transformed life, is the final word on God's covenant commitment to physical life.

The conclusion raised by these obvious, homely thoughts (and everything in God's speech is like that – there is nothing philosophical, technical or specialist) is that such a creation witnesses to its Creator who is covenant-keeping, purposeful and reliable. Therefore can we really believe he would be less than that in his dealings with us?

Creation displays delight, humour, surprise. Our meditation on the hymn to wisdom (Job 28) prepared the way for this observation: wisdom like a high-spirited child delights to sport with the human family in the playground of the world (Proverbs 8:22–31). Here 'the morning stars sang together and all the angels shouted for joy' (Job 38:7). Why did God create? For the joy of it.

Surely this is why we are shown strange and comic creatures such as the ostrich who has the last laugh, however stupid and ugly she is, because of her terrific acceleration and her kick like a bazooka (39:13–18). And what are we to make of the hippopotamus (40:15–24), or the crocodile who so intrigued God that it takes the whole of chapter 41 to sketch its character! Nature is one of God's languages and he allows it to speak on his behalf. Look at the way children react to these creatures when they see them; they are fascinated and frightened, awestruck and amused. The hippopotamus and the crocodile are gorgeously eccentric, odd and different. Can you seriously look a hippopotamus or a crocodile in the eye and still believe you understand God's ways? To paraphrase Job 41:5, we can no more tame the thoughts and ways of this God than a little girl could lead a crocodile on a piece of string.

Creation can play the fool. There seems to be a lot going on out there which is simply for the extravagant fun of it, a show put on for our delight and deserving our careful respect.

> ... God be with the clown –
> who ponders this tremendous scene –
> this whole experiment of green –
> As if it were his own!
>
> *Emily Dickinson*[5]

Look at the odd-ball characters in the animal (and in the human!) domain and we can surely hear the Maker's chuckle.

> A good laugh is a sign of love; it may be said to give
> us a glimpse of, or a first lesson in, the love that
> God bears for every one of us ... we surely expect
> this little creature called laughter to lapse suddenly
> into silence and nothingness when it enters the
> eternal halls of heaven. The Bible corrects that
> impression. It actually makes laughter the image and
> likeness of God's feelings towards what goes on
> here below [Psalm 2].
>
> *Karl Rahner*[6]

And on this same theme of surprise, humour, delight, Barry Ulanov writes about how laughter can invade our prayer life:[7]

> We can come close enough in our lightness of spirit to see and enjoy the playful aspect of the divine. We laugh in our prayer. God must long for a funny story, we think, instead of still another lugubrious hymn or turgid meditation, still another solemn promise, still another tortured, pompous confession in which even our sins are matters of pride. One of the most lethal perversions of religion is to present it as so constantly dreary, so dull and joyless. What, after all, is the purpose of the life of the spirit – to show ourselves off as small, mean and boastful, or to glorify God? 'The glorification of God,' Moultmann reminds us, 'lies in the demonstrative joy of existence' . . . any prayer that bores us must surely tax even an infinite patience.

Creation witnesses to God's power and majesty. Look at the great war-horse (Job 39:19–25) in its glory, exulting in its strength as it charges into the enemy lines. If the ostrich is the clown, the battle-horse is the warrior-king. We might laugh at the ostrich and throw stones at the wild donkey but it would not be wise to heckle the great horse. He appears to us huge, fleet, strong, savage and beautiful. God's description is so excited and tense, so admiring of the magnificence of the horse that our imaginations can easily see in it a potent icon of its Maker's own power and majesty.

And then there are 'the laws of the heavens' (38:31–33; Genesis 1:14–15). Job is unable to position the stars in the right place at the right season: they belong to 'God's dominion' and are witness to his power and majesty. The results of astronomy help us to believe in that power even when it is impossible to imagine.

When we have become ready to accept without demur the statement that the temperature at the centre of a star may be something like one-thousand-million degrees centigrade and that the atoms of which it is composed have been stripped not only of their electrons but also of particles from their nuclei under pressure of the order of 100,000 million million pounds per square inch, it hardly seems reasonable to cavil at the ultimate transformation which Christianity postulates simply on the ground that it is difficult to imagine.

E L Mascall[8]

Creation points to God's irrepressible freedom. The hawk and the eagle soar and glide (Job 39:26–30). The wild donkey and wild ox (vv5–12), famously unbiddable, mock man's attempt to break them in for domestic service. The crocodile – 'If you lay a hand on him, you will remember the struggle and never do it again!' (41:8) – is untameable, provoking God's delicious sarcasm, 'Will he keep begging you for mercy?' (41:3).

Learn the lesson. We will never catch God in the net of our theories, rules and schemes. We cannot tame him, domesticate him, render him harmless and sweet, train him to do our bidding.

Creation celebrates God's respect for distinctiveness. As the carnival troops by, each performer is distinct and different. The horse is not the hippopotamus, the hawk is not an ostrich. And Job, a human being, is different again. Of each species, at creation God said it was 'good', meaning, 'This is just what I want you to be.' Gerard Manley Hopkins strikingly illustrated this truth: 'As kingfishers catch fire, dragonflies draw flame', each creature gives out that special quality given to it by its Maker. The kingfisher's azure back and wings radiate fire when touched by sunlight. The dragonfly seems to shoot flame out of a blowpipe. Hopkins goes on, '. . . what I do is me: for that I came'. In one of his sermons he expands the idea (see also Psalm 148):

> The birds sing to him, the thunder speaks of his terror, the lion is like his strength, the sea is like his greatness, the honey like his sweetness; they are something like him, they make him known, they tell of him, they give him glory . . .

Because God creates each thing in its own distinctive nature within the great scheme of creation that exists to mirror forth the glory of God, Job can be absolutely sure that God intends the best for him, too. However strange and difficult his experiences have been, the world calls out that 'in all things God works for the good of those who love him'(Romans 8:28), where 'good' means that we are healed and restored to make God known in our own unique way, true to our nature, giving out the special quality given to it by our Maker-Redeemer.

The world is the 'loveliest reflection of his face'. Where and how else are we able to look on the dazzling beauty of the Lord? Not by gazing straight at him. If even the headlights of an oncoming car at night are capable of 'blinding us', what hope have we of surviving the sight of God's beauty? 'The brilliance of the light had blinded me,' said Paul who needed to be led around like a child after his experience of seeing the Lord (Acts 22:11).

We have verbal descriptions – God is adorned with glory and splendour, and clothed in honour and majesty (Job 40:10) – but using such words is like trying to describe the light spectrum to someone who is colour blind. These are not qualities we often see in our daily lives.

Yet we *can* look at him and survive with our eyesight intact. We can gaze at his loveliness reflected in creation as 'in a mirror dimly' until the moment when we are transformed and able to see him 'face to face' (1 Corinthians 13:12, RSV). St John of the Cross (1542–1591), who delighted to apply the imagery of the natural world to God, wrote:

> Rare gifts he scattered
> As through these woods and groves he passes apace
> Turning, as on he sped,
> And clothing every place
> With loveliest reflection of his face . . .
> The creatures all around
> Speak of thy graces as I pass them by.
> Each deals a deeper wound
> And something in their cry
> Leaves me so raptured that I fain would die.

Has ever such haunting expression been given to the sense that the beauty of the natural world is both an effect and a reflection of the uncreated beauty of its Maker?

However, not everyone can see it that way. God in nature has died for modern man. We have nature-as-god, nature-mysticism of many kinds and nature-instead-of-God. To see that 'the world is charged with the grandeur of God' (Manley Hopkins) requires healed eyesight. It calls for what Jesus called the 'good-eye', meaning the straight, healthy, sincere, uncorrupted, vision of a child who can see without cynicism and without endless analysis of what he is observing. In our culture we analyse not to adore but to gain mastery. Yet it is, as Emily Dickinson said, a mistake to slit open the skylark to look for the song.

Observing the world with the good eye, 'your whole body will be full of light' (Matthew 6:22) as our eyes by looking learn to see and we discern the loveliness of the Lord in his world-mirror. It will happen when we allow God and his creation to honour each other mutually, to reveal the truth about each other. 'Till you can sing and rejoice and delight in God, as misers do in gold, and kings in sceptors, you never enjoy the world' (Traherne).

One last thought: creation goes on with its business of radiating the love and the loveliness of God even when nobody is on hand to witness it! Its calling and meaning and reason for existing is glorifying God. God has not answered Job's questions. Instead he takes Job's arm and says, 'Look, the world is bloom, festal, a holy feast. It is not blind, dumb, a vain jest. The dance moves the world, not chance. Now, trust me with the outcome of your life.'

A SECOND INTERPRETATION

Job 38 – 42:6

That God allows his creation to speak for him accounts to some extent for Job's reaction. As creation's parable dances around him it triggers the dramatic realisation that he has been altogether wrong about God (Job 42:1–3). It explains also his tremendous embarrassment at the way he has been haranguing God all along.

Yet this does not adequately explain Job's utter self-abasement and prostrate repentance: 'Therefore I despise myself and repent in dust and ashes' (v 6). Something much more than acknowledgement of error and submission to God's superior power and intelligence is going on in that cry.

When Isaiah and Paul encountered the divine transcendant majesty, they found in it powerful reasons for intellectual humility on our part. Thus in the metaphor of the potter and the clay: ' " . . . who resists his will?" But who are you, O man, to talk back to God? "Shall what is formed say to him who formed it, 'Why did you make me like this?' " Does not the Potter have the right . . .' (Romans 9:19–21). 'As the heavens are higher than the earth, so are my ways higher than your ways . . .' (Isaiah 55:8, 9). Both these passages make an appeal to the reasonableness of the reader. Both are rational conclusions that the intellect is unable to penetrate God's mind.

It is different with Job. He adds no reasons, deductions or solutions onto God's answer, only his gasp of discovery: 'My ears had heard of you but now my eyes have seen you' (Job 42:5). Something happens in that strange moment to overwhelm his mind. Whatever it is, it resolves his difficulties with God instantaneously and sets them in a wholly new perspective, relieving his exhausted mind of all its stress.

> Seeing God, Job forgets all he wanted to say, all he thought he would say if he could but see him.
>
> *George Macdonald*[1]

What is this tremendous event? What has Job seen? How does this discovery heal his anguish and outrage?

We need to explore a second interpretation of God's answer.

Under the impact of the divine presence

We have already seen the various aspects of creation as a series of arguments and reasons why Job should trust God for the outcome of his life, however painful his experiences. In this second way of understanding God's answer I am suggesting that Job did not merely reconstruct his ideas about the justice and love of God; he also felt the overpowering impact of God's personality and this left him weak and dizzy with awe but completely at peace.

> God reveals His presence:
> Let us now adore Him,
> And with awe appear before Him.
> > God is in His Temple:
> All within keep silence,
> Prostrate lie with deepest reverence.
> > Him alone
> > God we own,
> Him our God and Saviour
> Praise His name forever!
>
> *Gerhard Teersteegen (1697–1769)*

Awe and reverence in the presence of infinite mystery and

infinite majesty. Notice how in Teersteegen's hymn the sight of God is followed similarly by exclamations of self-abandonment to God and his glory.

We have seen how the Hekhalot hymn-writer struggled to convey the wondrous-terrifying presence of God (page 24) but abandoned the attempt with the helpless warning, '. . . whoever glimpses his beauty immediately melts away' (literally: he is emptied out like a ladle). The prophets testified to similar effects: they are stunned, speechless, drained, shattered. Pascal left a cryptic note, dated 23 November 1654, time 10.30 pm, which referred to an encounter with God lasting for about two hours, expressed in the single word, 'Fire'.

In their different ways, these worshippers strove to tell of their dangerous, but fascinating, encounters with the numinous mystery that is God, in which they 'saw' things previously known to them only theoretically and at second-hand: 'My ears had heard of you but now my eyes have seen you'. Herein lies the final answer to our questions about divine providence and the problem of innocent suffering. And this experience is not the special property of spiritual high-flyers. Job was hardly in a serene and receptive state of mind when God broke through to him: 'Oh, that I had someone to hear me! I sign my own defence – let the Almighty answer me; let my accuser put his indictment in writing'(Job 31:35). He expected explanations, and God sent the fire of his presence into his mind. There can be no doubt we were created for nothing less than an experience of God like that – real, intense, personal, revelatory – in which our questions are dissolved in the fire of his presence. Indeed, if we will not have the fire of God we are doomed to be left with our boredom, the curse of the contemporary Western way of life.

I love Don Marquis' story about Archy, a cockroach who lives in the office typewriter and types his philosophical observations on life in free verse. In 'the lesson of the moth', Archy, street-wise and disillusioned, reports:[2]

> i was talking to a moth
> the other evening
> he was trying to break into
> an electric light bulb
> and fry himself on the wires

Archy tries to talk the moth out of this ambition. The moth answers:

> we get bored with the routine
> and crave beauty
> and excitement
> fire is beautiful
> and we know that if we get
> too close it will kill us
> but what does that matter
> it is better to be happy
> for a moment
> and be burned up with beauty . . .
> it is better to be a part of beauty
> for one instant and then cease to
> exist than to exist forever
> and never be a part of beauty

And Archy continues:

> . . . before i could argue him
> out of his philosophy
> he went and immolated himself
> on a patent cigar lighter
> i do not agree with him
> myself i would rather have
> half the happiness and twice
> the longevity
> but at the same time i wish
> there was something i wanted
> as badly as he wanted to fry himself

archy

The answer to people who seem hell-bent on self-destruction through drugs, sex, or high speed living, is probably not to make Archy's mistake of trying to argue them out of their philosophy only to leave them with this intolerable secular *ennui*. Perhaps a determination to go out with a bang is no worse than the willingness to die inch by inch through boredom. However ...

> Suppose you can be a part of beauty not merely for one instant but forever; suppose you can have *all* the happiness and *all* the longevity, then could any effort be too great in order to attain this end? Suppose you can enjoy the very life of God, and suppose this flame is one that does not destroy but transforms and transfigures, that gives not death but life ... [3]

This kind of encounter with God is not escapism or romanticism in place of hard thinking and sacrificial action in a world where, in spite of all our science and technology, vast numbers of men, women and children live on the edge of famine, uneducated and in poor health.

> Only those Christians who are most deeply aware of the utter transcendence of God will be able to interpret to modern atheists their own experience of existence with some hope of success ... God's majesty must stand out as the unchangeable background on which the diverse mysteries of Christ are outlined ... the meaning of our time is that God should be exalted higher above contemporary man who himself occupies a higher position than before, and that man thus exalted should in his turn fall down more humbly before this infinitely exalted Lord. Christians must be more intensely on fire with the love of God!
>
> *Balthasar*[4]

In the fire of God's presence we will find the vision which

our exhausted world longs for, even when it does not call it by that name.

So we must look again at God's strange answer which is 'a solution only God could give, a solution which does not solve the perplexity but buries it under the tide of a fuller life and joy in God. It is a solution as broad as Job's life and not merely the measure of his understanding' (Davidson).[5]

'Out of the storm' (Job 38:1)

It was not the way the wisdom teachers would have expected God to communicate with them. The whirlwind does not suggest intimacy, approachability, or encourage the recipient to feel himself in harmony with the divine wisdom that directs creation. It is different from the gentle 'still, small voice' (1 Kings 19:12). The storm belongs to the older tradition of Sinai, the Song of Deborah (Judges 5:4,5) and the Psalms (18:7–15; 29). It alerts us to the reality of our situation: we are out of our depth; we could easily be blown away by God showing himself like this; it is beyond our control.

Symbols of the mystery

> Glory be to God for dappled things . . .
>
> All things counter, original, spare, strange;
> Whatever is fickle, freckled (who knows how?)
> With swift, slow; sweet, sour; adazzle, dim;
> He fathers-forth whose beauty is past change:
> Praise him.
>
> *Gerard Manley Hopkins*[6]

The eagle suggests an elusive majesty. The wild donkey and wild ox contradict our neat ideas of constructive purpose. Yet their remote, inaccessible existence is fascinating and we have to admire their total indifference to our human world. The weird ostrich, the joker in the pack, also seems to deny intelligent, useful design by her bizarre behaviour. Indeed, the point is stressed that God deliberately made the big bird scatty! (Job 39:17).

As for the crocodile and the hippopotamus, they express more than the other creatures the downright stupendousness, the wholly incomprehensible character of the eternal creative power, how incalculable and 'wholly other' it is. It mocks at all conceiving, but can yet stir the mind to its depths, fascinate and over brim the heart . . . The crocodile and hippopotamus are 'monsters' but the monstrous is just the 'mysterious' in the gross form. We normally observe these animals when they are safe behind zoo bars, which diminishes the impact of their mystery! Yet clearly God intends a special significance for them since such a large part of his answer is devoted to their detailed description. Their 'mystery', or rather the mystery of which they are symbols, takes on a startling dimension once we restore to both their mythological names.

A message from Behemoth and Leviathan

Behemoth (the hippopotamus, 40:15) and Leviathan (the crocodile, 41:1) were the primeval monsters of chaos, Tiamat and Kingu, in Babylonian mythology. In Jewish apocalyptic, Behemoth and Leviathan were 'cast the one into the abyss of the sea, and the other into the dry land of the wilderness . . . These two monsters . . . will be food for all the righteous who remain'. Scripture agrees: 'In that day, the Lord . . . will slay the monster of the sea' (Leviathan, Isaiah 27:1).

This imagery is central to the message of the book of *Revelation* where the dragon (Satan) makes use of his two agents, the beast from the sea (Rome) and the beast out of the earth (the local puppet government) who carry out the dragon's wishes (Revelation 13). As prophesied in Isaiah, the dragon is fatally wounded (Revelation 12) and, in its death throes, creates all possible mayhem in the present age because 'he knows that his time is short' (Revelation 12:12). If we enter into the apocalyptic imagination as we read these scriptures, we will realise that there is a dynamic flow going on between these symbols and images as they feed and draw on each other.

When the Messiah comes again, Behemoth and Leviathan will be fed to the 'birds of the air' and 'beasts of the earth', signifying that God's marvellous purposes for creation are triumphing over the powers of chaos and destruction (see Ezekiel 32:2–10; Psalm 74:12–15; Revelation 19:19–21).

Thus in his answer to Job God incorporates, in the hippopotamus and the crocodile, potent symbols of the spiritual conflict which constantly threatens creation. Any picture of the world without this spiritual dimension would be hopelessly unreal and naive. The two monsters in the midst of nature symbolise conflict with hostile powers, which climaxes when 'having disarmed the powers and authorities, [Christ makes] a public spectacle of them, triumphing over them by the cross' (Colossians 2:14,15). Behemoth and Leviathan represent a creation in need of redemption, and therefore a Creator who must also be a Redeemer. The two functions of creating and redeeming meet and are satisfied in Christ Jesus. He is our Creator, and he became our Redeemer. He can be our Redeemer because he is our Creator. Thus the two monsters are evidence of the rich, complex, deep, mysterious way in which creation is trying to communicate something of God's purposes to us. How else could we know something of the awfulness of the crucifixion of God's Son if nature had not 'painted it in' for us: the sun looked away in grief, the earth shook, the rocks split, the graves gave up their dead, the curtain of the temple in Jerusalem split from top to bottom (Luke 23:44–46; Matthew 27:50–53).

Leviathan and Behemoth, creatures of chaos, also bring to our attention another creature not specifically mentioned in God's answer, yet implicit in everything that is said. This creature is 'time', or 'history', the unfolding of

God's purposes within time: 'I know that you can do all things; no plan of yours can be thwarted' (Job 42:2). The creatures of chaos appear in other forms: in Daniel's vision (Daniel 7:2–7) their symbolism points to the way God's purposes are fulfilled in the crises of history. Daniel's four ferocious beasts, all teeth and claws and insatiable appetite, arise from the sea, the great reservoir of human evil, their spawning ground. For Daniel they represent the four great empires of his world, for us the monstrous powers of evil in our own times, the Hitlers, the Stalins, the Pol Pots.

In *Revelation* the beasts are not eaten but transformed into symbols of the cosmos, 'ransomed, healed, restored, forgiven', before a sea cleansed and tamed (Revelation 4:6). Such transformation is creation's covenanted destiny, secured by Christ, even though at this moment the various cousins of Behemoth and Leviathan, like Daniel's monsters, are stirring in the depths of the sea.

> In that day,
>   the Lord will punish with his sword,
>   his fierce, great and powerful sword,
> Leviathan, the gliding serpent,
>   Leviathan the coiling serpent;
>   he will slay the monster of the sea.
>
> *Isaiah 27:1*

God's answer breaks over Job, drenching his spirit with the strangeness and fascination of incomprehensible mystery and awe-inspiring majesty. He can only gasp a few words (like a drowning swimmer breaking the surface), a helpless cry of recognition at his first sight of God. In this moment his anguish is relieved even if his complaints are not answered in the usual sense of the word.

What has happened is so fundamental to the purpose of the book of *Job* that we must explore it further. We can do this by looking a little closer at some of the terms by which we have tried to describe the encounter.

The numinous

This word was coined to convey the inexpressible, the awe and reverence sensed in the presence of infinite mystery and infinite majesty.

We find the numinous when we read Isaiah 6 and feel the prophet's sense of being utterly overpowered by God. If we do not, then no amount of 'preaching, singing, telling', in Luther's phrase, can help us. People testify to the numinous stealing quietly into their consciousness in a dawning awareness; or as a detonation, a sudden explosive eruption. It may come in a hushed, trembling, speechless humility; or intoxicated, ecstatic joy.

Isaiah experienced the numinous in the temple. Since God had given to creation the task of answering for him, Job presumably sensed it in the open air; perhaps while walking in the countryside he heard a voice saying, 'Look.'

In his fascinating book *Religious Experience Today* David Hay gives further examples of similar encounters with the numinous presence of God, under the title 'The Vividness of the Spirit'.[7] One person tells of an experience while listening to the music of Bach.

> A friend persuaded me to go to Ely Cathedral to hear a performance of Bach's B Minor Mass. I had heard the work, indeed I know Bach's choral works pretty well. I was sitting towards the back of the nave. The Cathedral seemed to be very cold. The music thrilled me . . . until we got to the great Sanctus. I find this experience difficult to define. It was primarily a warning. I was frightened. I was trembling from head to foot, and wanted to cry. Actually I think I did. I heard no 'voice' except the music; I saw nothing; but the warning was very definite. I was not able to interpret this experience satisfactorily until I read – some months later – Rudolph Otto's 'The Idea of the Holy'. Here I found it: the 'numinous', I was before the Judgement

Seat. I was being 'weighed in the balance and found wanting'. This is an experience I have never forgotten.

Another encounter comes during prayer at a time of particular openness to God.

I came to the end of my tether one day and realised that only God could help me. I prayed and as I could not feel any contact made myself persevere. I realised my prayers all my life had only been lip service. I spent more and more time each day in prayer, and one day I suddenly felt the breakthrough. I knew I was in touch with a spiritual being. My prayer for help really came from my heart, mind and soul, for the very first time. After some time, I felt a warm glow on my head. Very slowly it spread until my whole being was suffused with it. I kept my eyes closed so don't know if there was any visual accompaniment. Gradually, the glow subsided and I rose to my feet. Then the strangest thing happened. On both my shoulders was firm pressure as of unseen hands. I was guided to a bookcase and my right hand involuntarily reached out and I selected a book. I opened it and from the pages fell a text cut from a newspaper . . . 'All things whatsoever ye shall ask in prayer, believing, ye shall receive.'

Another common condition in which the numinous deeply affects people is when a person is open to the wonder of creation as Job is. The following describes a childhood experience.

One such place has a significance for me beyond all others. A mile or so from ——, the heath fell away to the estuary of the [river] ——, a few sparsely clothed Scotch firs along its banks. To the left, —— Church crouched austerely above the few cottages that are the remnant of the flourishing medieval port. And in the far distance, beyond the firs, gleaming against the dark sky, the white fleck of ―――― Lighthouse. This scene, lovely enough, but not uniquely so, became at some point a window through which my childish sensibilities (I must have been about four at the time) glimpsed a still beauty that I have since come to recognise as the most powerful and awesome experience of my life, different not just in intensity, but in kind, from any other . . .

The next instance that David Hay describes came in what he calls 'moments of quiet reflection' and, again, the experience comes in early childhood.

My father used to take all the family for a walk on Sunday evenings. On one such walk, we wandered across a narrow path through a field of high, ripe corn. I lagged behind, and found myself alone. Suddenly, heaven blazed on me. I was enveloped in golden light. I was conscious of a presence, so kind, so loving, so bright, so consoling, so commanding, existing apart from me but so close. I heard no sound. But words fell into my mind quite clearly – 'Everything is all right. Everybody will be all right.'

The next encounter was experienced while listening to a sermon, describing the effect on someone of the preaching of an evangelist.

I listened to the sermon and it was as if some power beyond myself took hold of me and spoke to me. The words spoken seemed for me alone and when we were asked to go forward to dedicate our lives to Christ *nothing* and I mean *nothing* could have held me back. I wish to impress very strongly on you that it was not emotional feeling alone or mass hysteria as some say. I was just drawn by a power beyond myself and I felt my great need. Afterwards I felt a great peace and joy that I can't put into words. It was, and still is, a miracle to me.

The next is an unusual and touching example of an encounter with the numinous while watching children.

About this time I began working part-time among mentally and physically badly handicapped children. There was a particular child who was totally helpless in mind and body, and in constant pain. One morning I saw him and felt more than usually distressed and disturbed by him. On my way home, I was thinking about him in relation to the Creator of things (God?) – and suddenly saw everything in its true proportion – the smallness of man's life and lifespan and the immense otherness of the force outside us. I can still recapture the extraordinary impact of this idea as it came to me then (by great concentration) but I can never adequately express it.

We discover the numinous when we read the Bible, and the life and power of God's word leap from the page.

Once, when I had been reading John 12, verses 24 and 25, 'I tell you, most solemnly, unless a wheat grain falls on the ground and dies, it remains only a single grain; but if it dies, it yields a rich harvest. Anyone who loves his life loses it; anyone who hates his life in this world will keep it for eternity.' And I went for a walk in some pine woods alone. It was a glorious spring day and I stopped for a bit under a pine tree and looked at things. Quite suddenly those verses became full of a new depth of meaning and everything I saw in nature around me glowed with this meaning and truth for the whole of life, mine included.

The last example describes an encounter when the person was alone in church.

For me there is something extraordinary about the stillness of ancient churches, especially those in remote places. They seem to symbolise the most profound part of us that is waiting to be rediscovered. Once, sitting in the northernmost of our great churches, surrounded by the red glow of the ancient stone, I found myself opening a Bible at the place where God asks Job, 'Where were you when I laid the foundations of the earth?' The total context engendered such a sense of religious awe, that the only adequate release was tears.

These encounters with the numinous appear to have two things in common. The first is the mysterious sense of something that was there all the time, but hidden, suddenly revealed. The second is a characteristic awed silence following each experience of revelation.

Numinous silence

This denotes the moment when God is in the midst of either a congregation or an individual's inner life. 'Be a standing majesty in the midst of us,' George Herbert prayed. The Lord visits his people and there is a silence that allows this revelation to happen. The silence is also the effect of the revelation, and is therefore a sacramental time when God is recognised and received by the worshipper.

But the Lord is in his holy temple;
let all the earth be silent before him
Habakkuk 2:20

> God reveals his presence . . .
> All within keep silence,
> Prostrate lie with deepest reverence.
>
> *Teersteegen*

Job waits, silent and prostrate. He has 'seen' the glory of the Lord, which encourages him to cast himself upon his mercy and grace, his forgiveness and restoration. It is the overwhelming impact of the numinous presence which prepares him for the next stage of silent communion with God and a further enlargement of his inner life to receive more and more of him.

Approaching the unapproachable

> God, the blessed and only Ruler, the King of kings and Lord of lords, who alone is immortal and who lives in unapproachable light, whom no-one has seen or can see. To him be honour and might for ever. Amen.
>
> *1 Timothy 6:15,16*

It is plain that Job is greatly affected by his realisation of the sheer difference in quality between God and himself (Job 42:3).

We have used words like 'incomprehensible' and 'inconceivable' to express the reality that God is beyond the grasp of our minds, yet we are not prevented from attempting to get our minds around him. 'Unapproachable' on the other hand places God beyond even the possibility of our reach or our investigation.

In his loving kindness God mediates himself to us through Jesus his Son, who humanises our contact with God and renders it 'safe' to receive God the Holy Spirit into our bodies. We can gaze upon 'the light of the knowledge of the glory of God' but only 'in the face of Jesus Christ' (2 Corinthians 4:6). Direct exposure to the unapproachable light would blast us into oblivion. God knows the impotence of our nature, the narrowness and meagreness of our perceptions. The unbearable intensity of his unapproachable light is filtered through Christ to us.

Yet how foolish we are when we act irreverently and in an over-familiar manner, as if the softened, filtered, mediated light is that 'wholly other' unapproachable light in which God dwells.

Unapproachable and yet irresistibly fascinating.

Fascination

Let us continue to explore Job's state of mind at the moment of his encounter with the unapproachable light. We must speculate but in a way that is supported by the recorded experiences of many worshipping believers.

Unlike Archy's moth who sought the flame for one sizzling, annihilating split-second of glory which justified its existence, the Christian longs to possess God and to be possessed by him because that transaction burns into eternal life and joy.

> O that I could tell you what the heart feels, how it burns and is consumed inwardly! Only I find no words to express it. I can but say: might but one little drop of what I feel fall into hell, hell would be transformed into a paradise.
>
> *Catherine of Genoa*

New Testament Christians agree in their descriptions of that 'burning into life' sensation for which they also could not find words:

> Though you have not seen [Jesus Christ], you love him; and even though you do not see him now, you believe in him and are filled with an inexpressible and glorious joy . . .
>
> *1 Peter 1:8*

The great Jonathan Edwards, who very closely observed the 'vividness of the Spirit' in people's lives during the eighteenth century Awakening in New England, also concluded that the authentic experience of God is beyond describing:

> The conceptions which the saints have of the loveliness of God, and that kind of delight which they experience in it, are quite peculiar and entirely different from anything which a natural man can possess or of which he can form any proper notion.

We were created and re-created in the Holy Spirit for the fire of that experience. Yet inevitably, because of what we are, and who God is in unapproachable light, there is a profound sense of unworthiness when we come into the divine presence.

Atonement and cleansing from sin

Job is overwhelmed by feelings of uncleanness induced by the numinous presence of God. Isaiah similarly: 'Woe to me! I am ruined! For I am a man of unclean lips and I live among a people of unclean lips, and my eyes have seen the King, the Lord Almighty'. So, too, Peter: 'Go away from me Lord; I am a sinful man!' There is nothing considered or worked-out in their response. In each case it is an involuntary, reflexive cry, as when we pick up something which is too hot. The effect of the presence of God is a spontaneous flinching on our part away from his unbearable holiness. The result is an instinctive self-criticism which extends to the society in which we are placed: 'I live among a people of unclean lips'. In that moment we re-evaluate ourselves, our environment and of course, by contrast and comparison, the glorious holiness of God. Indeed, the focus of our attention is upon the divine glory.

> For you alone are the Holy One,
> you alone are the Lord,
> you alone are the Most High,
> Jesus Christ,
> with the Holy Spirit,
> in the glory of God the Father. Amen.
>
> *From the Gloria, The Alternative Service Book*[8]

This reaction is not a natural process but the work of the Holy Spirit in people who are 'in the Spirit' (Revelation 1:10–17). The result is the realisation that we are simply not worthy to survive the presence of the All Holy God, while at the same time we know we cannot exist without him. Like the centurion we would say, 'I do not deserve to have you come under my roof' (Luke 7:1–10), and yet we must have his healing. We feel that Christ's holiness would be defiled by contact with our unclean lives, yet he must come close or we are lost. We long for atonement, for the expiation of our sins, for God's outraged holiness to be satisfied by his love, for the guilt of our sin to be lifted and the defilement of our sins to be cleansed. Thus at the centre of our encounter with the holy, numinous presence of God is the atoning cross of Christ:

> God is light; in him there is no darkness at all . . . if we walk in the light, as he is in the light, we have fellowship with one another, and the blood of Jesus, his Son, purifies us from all sin.
>
> *1 John 1:5–7*

> This is love: not that we loved God, but that he loved us and sent his Son as an atoning sacrifice for our sins.
>
> *1 John 4:10*

And love, says one of the mystics, is nothing else than quenched wrath.

THAT FIRST QUESTION AT LAST

Job 42

So the story has returned to the original question that triggered the *Job* drama – Does Job fear God for nothing (1:9)? – not by coming full circle but, as it were, by way of a spiral staircase reaching a higher level. Whatever selfish motives Satan had suspected in Job, it is obvious now even to this hateful demonic critic that if ever a man loved God for his own sake and 'for nothing' it is Job, prostrate in utter self-abandonment, claimed in the depth of his being by the mystery he cannot explain. In that moment Job foreshadows the Son of God – Jesus the second Adam, the true Man – who on behalf of his human family loved and obeyed the Father, thus completely vindicating God's wisdom and purposes in ever creating humankind at all.

Therefore, when Christ came into the world, he said:

'Sacrifice and offering you did not desire,
   but a body you prepared for me;
with burnt offerings and sin offerings
   you were not pleased.
Then I said, "Here I am – it is written about me
   in the scroll –
I have come to do your will, O God." '
                                        Hebrews 10:5–7

Not that Job can now walk away 'answered-fulfilled-satisfied'. He has done no more than approach the threshold of the presence of the One who dwells in unapproachable light. His life from now on will advance deeper and deeper into that mystery, for he has discovered that the 'answers' we seek are found there. His awesome encounter with God, his response of complete humility and renunciation, have produced a man who has shifted the weight of his being outside himself as it were, and he is free to know the boundless joy of seeking God.

Conclusions (Job 42:7–17)

Some of the commentators are uneasy with the epilogue. After the tough, austere realities of the book they find it too neat, too much like the happy-ever-afters of fairy tales. However, until this point in the poetic drama, in which very bad things happen to a very good man, there are too many loose ends for it to be left without a summing up. We look to Job's God to deliver a conclusion that will bring out of the story a message for our own struggles. The epilogue does exactly that.

He spoke 'what is right' about God

Satan's challenge in the opening episode was about the way in which a man who spoke so well of God in the good times will speak of him when his fortunes change. Here Job is publicly honoured for his integrity – he has 'spoken of me what is right' (Job 42:7) – which, when we recall some of Job's terrible outbursts against God, is a surprisingly generous thing for God to say.

However, Job's tenacious seeking after the truth, his unshakeable conviction that he must 'flee to the God from whom he was in flight' was far more honouring to God than the conventional arguments of his friends. They believed they were making out the best possible case for God, when in fact they were simply distorting reality. How God must have loved the bizarre sight of an outraged Job defending God from God's defenders! (13:7–11). His anger was far more honouring than their flatteries, and God loved him for it.

We know from God's answer that he did not approve of Job's arguments, and neither did he entirely disapprove of the friends' line of reasoning. Yet Job is loudly praised and Eliphaz, the oldest and intellectually most distinguished of the friends, is singled out for special criticism (v7). The difference is that Job, for all his confusions, tenaciously pursued the truth whereas Eliphaz and the others stayed safe and secure inside the bunker of their traditions. God admires a gritty fighter.

Beware those complacent counsellors!

Here is a delicious role-reversal as a warning to all of us who complacently advise others on the ways of God with his world. Eliphaz had earlier patronised Job with the promise of the power of intercession on behalf of sinners if only he would repent of his attacks on God (22:26–30). Now in this neat turning of the tables the 'sinner' intercedes for the 'saint' (vv8,9)! John Gibson says of Job's friends that God 'had to tell them to their faces that they were not defenders of the faith but stumbling blocks to the faithful'.

This is not to despise the resources of their orthodox wisdom tradition. The trouble came from the dangerous way they applied it so rigidly and with such impregnable assurance. Whereas Job was moving on in search of an answer which covered the facts of his life, they saw life through the filters of their theories. They must have been delighted and felt vindicated by God's great answer to Job. But here God publicly rebukes them for tinkering with reality in his name. The principle is that we should receive and handle revelation humbly, responsibly, with a prayerful, teachable and adoring mind, all the time prepared to see it afresh from 'altered perspectives' (see pages 40–41).

Be open to the old wisdom

Having exposed the champions of the old orthodoxy to public censure, the author of the epilogue reinstates wisdom with a symbolic gesture. Job fulfils the wisdom principle that God will bless the good person: 'the Lord made him prosperous again and gave him twice as much as he had before' (v10).

The rigid equation between suffering and sin, cause and effect, reaping and sowing, has been blown open by Job's own experiences of unmerited suffering. But having well and truly demonstrated the inadequacies of traditional wisdom when too narrowly interpreted and applied, we are now reminded that moral laws do operate in our lives and that there is indeed a correlation between what we think and do, and the effects of those choices on our lives.

While Eliphaz, Bildad, Zophar and Elihu were limited in their own interpretations of wisdom, we have nevertheless surely seen enough (from chapters 28, 38–41; Proverbs 8) to realise that wisdom stands where the paths meet beside the city gates, and at the entrances, calling out to all who would choose life (Proverbs 8).

At the moment, the model of Christian life, experience and worship which is carrying everything before it is the Corinthian-Charismatic one, for which we heartily thank God. But if we would live within the whole counsel of God, and for the sake of depth, balance and the art of living well, we will need to embrace also the model of wisdom described in these scriptures.

Satan wasn't asked to the party

Since Satan's challenge opened the drama, it is rather surprising that he was not summoned for a final confrontation with God, and with Job whose faithfulness vindicated God before all heaven.

In fact it is highly significant that he does not appear at the end. The value of Job's story to us it is that the cause of his suffering was unknown to him, just as ours is usually unknown to us. Satan's appearance here would have diminished the cosmic dilemma of evil in God's creation to the level of one person's set of experiences. Job stands for Everyman, and suffering is the basic human condition, 'born to trouble as surely as sparks fly upward' (Job 5:7).

The new prosperity – a sign of resurrection

Job has seen a vision of a living *Go'el*-Redeemer and the promise of life (19:25–27). Everything Job had ever known, all the terrible things that had shaken his life, are now caught up and radically transformed in a 'resurrection' experience. Here is grace, forgiveness and reconciliation (vv7–9), banqueting, teeming life, reunion, generosity, superabundance and loveliness (vv10–17). It will do very well as a metaphor of heaven and the sheer prodigality and limitless resources of resurrection life.

Finally, the presence

Job's strange story powerfully directs us to take the dilemma of our sufferings to God. He hints at how God makes himself available to us on this side of heaven while we walk by faith. He suggests the possibility that in such encounters with the living Lord our pain will be enfolded in love. God will himself be the answer. Yet there is still more to come:

> Now we see but a poor reflection as in a mirror;
> then we shall see face to face. Now I know in
> part; then I shall know fully, even as I am known.
> *1 Corinthians 13:12*

> I shall see your face; when I awake, I shall be satisfied
> with seeing your likeness.
> *Psalm 17:15*

With an anvil-ding
And with fire in him forge thy will
Or rather, rather then, stealing as Spring
Through him, melt him but master him still . . .
Make mercy in all of us, out of us all
Mastery, but be adored, but be adored King.

Gerard Manley Hopkins[1]

ACKNOWLEDGEMENTS

The wager

[1] Patrick Kavanagh, from 'The Devil', *The Complete Poems*, Goldsmith Press, Newbridge, Co. Kildare, Ireland, 1992. Copyright © Mr Peter Kavanagh.

[2] George Herbert (1593–1633), from 'Providence', *A Choice of George Herbert's Verse*, Faber & Faber 1967.

[3] Austin Farrer, *Said or Sung*, Faith Press 1960.

[4] William Shakespeare (1564–1616), from Sonnet 116.

[5] C S Lewis, from *The Screwtape Letters*, HarperCollins Publishers Limited 1982.

[6] Ann and Barry Ulanov, *Primary Speech – A psychology of prayer*, SCM Press 1985.

[7] 'Song at Daybreak', from *The Penguin Book of Hebrew Verse*, (ed. and trans.) T Carmi, (Allen Lane) 1981, p370, copyright © T Carmi 1981. Reproduced by permission of Penguin Books Limited.

[8] John Donne (1572–1631), from *Holy Sonnets*, xiv.

[9] Augustine (354–430), from *Confessions*, bk. x, ch. 6.

[10] Herbert, from 'Obedience'.

[11] John White, *The Race*, Inter-Varsity Press 1984.

[12] Farrer, *Commentary on Revelation*, 1964, by permission of Oxford University Press.

[13] 'The Face of God' and 'God's Robe of Glory', from *The Penguin Book of Hebrew Verse*, The Hekhalot Hymns, pp196/199, copyright © T Carmi 1981. Reproduced by permission of Penguin Books Limited. The Hekhalot Hymns are third and fourth century Hebrew devotional poems and hymns.

The lament
[1] Reprinted from *The Message of the Psalms* by Walter Brueggemann, copyright © 1984 Augsburg Publishing House. Used by permission of Augsburg Fortress (US).

[2] 'I am Who I Am' prayer – author unknown.

As sparks fly upward
[1] Farrer, *Saving Belief*, Hodder & Stoughton 1967.

[2] Farrer, from *The One Genius*, an anthology of his works selected by Richard Harries, SPCK 1987.

More deeply and more terribly
[1] Gerhard von Rad, *Wisdom in Israel*, SCM Press 1975.

[2] Herbert, 'Bitter-Sweet', *A Choice of George Herbert's Verse*.

We are mere yesterdays
[1] Emily Dickinson (1830–1886), Poem no. 695, *The Complete Poems of Emily Dickinson*, Faber & Faber.

Stepping-stones
[1] Dickinson, Poem no. 376, *The Complete Poems*.

[2] G K Chesterton, *The Essential G K Chesterton*, 1987, by permission of Oxford University Press.

[3] Walter Eichrodt, *Theology of the Old Testament*, vol. 2, SCM Press 1979.

[4] Immanuel of Rome, thirteenth century Hebrew poet.

Beyond the worm's-eye view
[1] John Gibson, *Job*, The Daily Study Bible Series, St Andrew Press 1985.

[2] See Hans Urs von Balthasar, *Truth is Symphonic*, Ignatius Press (US).

Let God be God
[1] Dickinson, Poem no. 1643, *The Complete Poems*.

[2] Farrer, *Said or Sung*.

[3] Farrer, *A Celebration of Faith*, Hodder & Stoughton 1970.

At the true heart and centre of things
[1] John Baillie, from 'Night Thoughts', *Christian Devotion*, 1962, by permission of Oxford University Press.
[2] Ulanov, *Primary Speech – A psychology of prayer.*
[3] Baillie, *Christian Devotion.*

We have a friend
[1] Solomon Ibn Gabriol (AD 1055), Jewish poet, from 'The Royal Crown'.
[2] James Torrance, from 'The vicarious humanity of Christ', *Incarnation*, T & T Clark.
[3] Gerard Manley Hopkins, *Sermons*, 1959, by permission of Oxford University Press.
[4] Hopkins, from 'As kingfishers catch fire, dragonflies draw flame', *The Poems*, 1978, by permission of Oxford University Press.

Life audit
[1] Von Rad, *Wisdom in Israel.*
[2] Herbert, from 'The Elixer', *A Choice of George Herbert's Verse.*
[3] Kavanagh, from 'The Self-Slaved', *The Complete Poems.*
[4] Kavanagh, from 'Canal Bank Wall', *The Complete Poems.*

Startling disclosures
[1] John Bunyan, *The Pilgrim's Progress.*
[2] Thomas F Torrance, *The Mediation of Christ*, T & T Clark 1992.

Ask around
[1] From Gustavo Gutierrez, *On Job: God-talk and the Suffering of the Innocent*, appears by kind permission of Orbis Books, Maryknoll, New York, USA, 1989.
[2] Robert Gordis, *The Book of Job: Commentary and New*

Translation, Jewish Theological Seminary of America 1978.
[3] George Steiner, *Bluebeard's Castle*, Faber & Faber.
[4] David J Bosch, *Transforming Mission*, appears by kind permission of Orbis Books, Maryknoll, New York, USA, 1991.

Restored for ministry
[1] Thomas F Torrance, *The Apocalypse Today*, James Clarke & Co 1960.

Handles
[1] Eric Lionel Mascall, *The Christian Universe*, Darton, Longman & Todd 1966.
[2] Robertson Davies, *What's bred in the bone*, Viking 1985 (first published by Macmillan Canada), p214, copyright © Robertson Davies 1985. Reproduced by kind permission of Penguin Books Limited.
[3] H H Rowley, *The Book of Job*, New Century Bible Series, Marshall, Morgan & Scott 1981.
[4] George Macdonald, from *George Macdonald – An anthology*, (ed.) C S Lewis, Geoffrey Bles, an imprint of HarperCollins Publishers Limited.

The 'poor man' takes centre-stage
[1] For further reading on the Isaiah Agenda, see Raymond Fung, *The Isaiah Vision: Ecumenical Strategy for Congregational Evangelism*, The World Council of Churches 1992.

The power of an adoring mind
[1] Bishop Hilary (fourth century), from Thomas F Torrance, *The Trinitarian Faith: Evangelical Theology of the Ancient Catholic Church*, T & T Clark 1988.

Where is wisdom?
[1] Hans Walter Wolff, *Anthropology of the Old Testament*, SCM Press 1974.

[2] T S Eliot, from 'The Rock', *Collected Poems 1909–1962*, Faber & Faber Limited. With permission of the Eliot Estate.

[3] Wolff, *Anthropology of the Old Testament*.

[4] Thomas Traherne (1637–1674), 'Thanksgiving for the glory of God's works'.

The answer

[1] *George Macdonald – An anthology.*

[2] Von Rad, *Wisdom in Israel*.

[3] Karl Barth, *Church Dogmatics*, vol.4 pt.3 (T & T Clark), quoted from *Wisdom in Israel*.

[4] Eugene Warren, from Thomas Howard, *Chance or the Dance?*, Ignatius Press (US) 1992.

[5] Dickinson, Poem no. 1333, *The Complete Poems*.

[6] Karl Rahner, *Belief Today*, Sheed & Ward 1973.

[7] Ulanov, *Primary Speech – A psychology of prayer*.

[8] Mascall, *The Christian Universe*.

A second interpretation

[1] *George Macdonald – An anthology.*

[2] Don Marquis, 'the lesson of the moth', *archy and mehitabel*, Faber & Faber 1994.

[3] Mascall, *The Christian Universe*.

[4] Balthasar, *Science, Religion and Christianity*, quoted from Mascall, *The Christian Universe*.

[5] A B Davidson, *Job*, Cambridge University Press 1962.

[6] Hopkins, from 'Pied Beauty', *The Poems*.

[7] David Hay, *Religious Experience Today: Studying the Facts*, Mowbray, a Cassell imprint, Wellington House, 125 Strand, London, 1990.

[8] *The Alternative Service Book 1980*, Copyright © The Central Board of Finance of the Church of England 1980.

That first question at last

[1] Hopkins, from 'The Wreck of the Deutschland', *The Poems*.

RECENT TITLES FROM
SCRIPTURE UNION

Closer to God: Practical help on your spiritual journey
Ian Bunting (Editor)
We are all on a journey through life, with God. For many
it is a struggle. What may help us? In this book members
of the Grove Spirituality Group write from personal
experience and from their understanding of the way
Christians have come closer to God down the centuries.

How to pray when life hurts
Roy Lawrence
Prayer makes a difference because God makes a difference.
Where can we find help when a situation seems beyond
hope? When a marriage is on the point of breakdown, a
disease is diagnosed as incurable, or an addiction is running out of control? Nothing is beyond the reach of Christ.
Nothing is beyond the healing difference he can make.
Whether we feel guilty or angry, fearful or under pressure,
this book offers practical help on *how* to pray when life
hurts.

Storytellers: Jesus through the eyes of people who knew
him
Andrew Brandon
On the way home from sentencing Jesus to death, Pilate
puts a phone call through to his wife . . . Dai and his wife
own a small hotel in the village. Nothing out of the
ordinary ever happens until a certain couple come to
stay . . . They call him Digit the Midget, the dwarf with the

pocket calculator brain, but after Jesus comes to dinner, Zacchaeus no longer feels like a zero . . .

Key events and characters of the New Testament are presented with startling freshness in this collection of monologues – 'an unusual and rewarding aid to personal devotion'.

Encounter with God in Job
Dennis Lennon
Moving through the Book of Job, Dennis Lennon explores the powerful themes that arise from Job's predicament and invites us to use these as a basis for meditating on God's involvement in the painful moments of life. God does not abandon Job or condemn him for his doubts. Instead Job is given a deeper insight into God's love and provision for this world.

Encounter with God in Hebrews
Joy Tetley
The complex Epistle to the Hebrews is often regarded as irrelevant to life in the twentieth century. Yet Hebrews gives us a vision of a God who is passionately involved with his people, and who challenges us to be open to an intimate relationship with him.

In this searching book, Joy Tetley invites us to look beyond the language and religious imagery of first-century Judaism to rediscover for ourselves the love which is timeless.

Both *Encounter with God in Hebrews* and *Encounter with God in Job* arise from series in the *Encounter with God* Bible reading notes. These series have been re-worked and expanded to book format but retain the distinctive *Encounter with God* approach to the Bible.

Thank God it's Monday: Ministry in the workplace
Mark Greene

Fun, fast and full of stories, this highly practical book looks at how we can make the most of the time we spend at work. It helps us to see our jobs, our co-workers and our bosses the way God sees them! How often do we end up limiting God's activities to the weekend? God is at work at work! At work in us. At work through us. At work in those we work with.

Just parenting
Christine Wright

For people awaiting the birth of a child or with under 5s, this book is a practical and humorous look at the skills and responsibilities involved in parenting.

Making Jesus known: Scripture Union stories from around the world
Michael Hews

Scripture Union is active in over 100 countries, spreading the good news to children, teens and adults. In this collection, fourteen staff members share some of their struggles, and tell us how they have seen God at work in their lives and in their ministries.

Ready for God? Expecting the Unexpected
R. T. Kendall

'Are you ready for God? Are you waiting for God to answer prayer? Are there prayers that you have long since taken off your prayer-request list because you were sure God wasn't going to answer them?'

Answered prayer is just one of many subjects R. T. Kendall explores in this book. Lively and challenging, it calls us to be ready for God however and whenever he may choose to appear.

Reaching families
Paul Butler

Statistics show that the family today is facing many changes and pressures, yet family is God's idea and intention. How can the people of God reflect the family nature of God in their life together and in the community around them? This book considers ways in which churches can reach out to families and to people living alone with the good news of Jesus Christ.

Living with a purpose
Nigel Scotland

'Riding on the early morning Piccadilly Underground I often used to look at the lines of newspapers gently bobbing up and down with the motion of the train and wonder if this was all there was to life . . .'

Nigel Scotland sets out to show that for Christians life has an extra dimension. In society, in the church, in our relationships, in our activities, if we are suffering and under stress, or if we are simply facing the challenges of every day, God gives us a purpose in living.